Steel Bolt Hacking

A Computerman's Guide to Lock Picking

By Douglas Chick

ISBN 0-9744630-1-9

Publisher –TheNetworkAdministrator.com
www.thenetworkadministrator.com

Editors
Ellen Chick
Erik Hansen
Schlaine Chudeusz

Technical
Joe Ritchey

Special Thanks to William Nett

for introducing me to the fun of lock picking

Thanks to Ted Dykstra

...and the crew of Colorado Hackers / Lockpickers at **dc719** for inspiring me to write this book. At Def Con 11 (2003), the dc719 crew introduced the first annual lock picking contest, LPCON. They can be reached at www.dc719.org

Thanks to Lockpicking101

I want to thank Mr. Picks at Lockpicking101 for putting together a great forum for lockpicking enthusiast.

Also thanks to Varjeal and his help as a locksmith, and for making the book a little more locksmith friendly and for the use of the terms and definitions used in this book.

And to Chuck Lemken for his suggestions on making the book a little easier to read for the beginner lock pick enthusiast.

All three are master lock picks and can be contacted at www.lockpicking101.com

Table of Contents

Introduction

Steel Bolt Hacking, or Lock Picking as it's most commonly known, is fast becoming a competitive sport among computer people. And it's far more than just picking locks. The 'sport' includes cracking combinations, push button door locks, magnetic key cards, and just about anything that has a lock to it. Lock picking sports groups are beginning to spring up in the U.S., the fastest growing groups are within the computer industry. Most computer people are fascinated with unlocking codes, bypassing security protocols and finding program vulnerabilities that can be exploited. Picking locks and cracking combinations are no different.

When I say that computer people have taken up the hobby of lock picking, I don't mean to suggest that they are breaking into people's homes or cars. Steel bolt hacking is nothing more than the challenge of picking locks in a legal and competitive manner. The only locks that are picked or combinations that are cracked are from locks that have been purchased for nothing more than the challenge of opening them with alternative methods. Some computer people have taken up lock picking as an alternative career that has led to becoming a part-time locksmith.

As far as I know, every computer person that has taken up lock picking or combination cracking has done so in a completely legal manner. The methods and styles of lock picking are passed on with an understanding that they are not to be used in committing illegal acts of breaking and entering. All the locks picked have been purchased and passed between other lock-picking enthusiasts to help sharpen their skills. Never have the skills and/or locks been used in a crime.

This book's objective isn't to turn anyone into a master criminal, or a minor one for that matter, but instead to help educate enough people to turn lock picking into a larger and more competitive sport. The techniques discussed in this book will require time, patience and practice. It can take up to 30 minutes to pick a lock, that is too much time for a criminal who can easily jimmy the door or drill out a pin in under 2 minutes. Time is always against a criminal, this is why they typically use brute force entry when committing a crime. Lock picking is an art that requires time to learn.

Who Should Read This Book

Who should read this book? If you have heard about the various lock picking sporting groups that are sweeping across the country and thought how interesting it might be to learn lock picking as a hobby, then you might want to read this book. If you've heard about the lock picking contests at the DefCon hacker's convention in Las Vegas and thought how cool it would be to join, then you might want to read this book. If you're a computer professional, computer hacker or an engineer, and you think that sci-fi conventions are too embarrassing to attend, but lock picking contests are awesome, then you are probably a geek, and should read this book.

This book teaches basic lock picking techniques and beyond. When you finish this book you will be capable of picking 75 percent of all locks in the world for hobby purposes, competition, or as some people who enjoy picking locks do, become locksmiths.

Lock picking is easy, fun, challenging and very addictive - well you know, just like computers are. There are certain similarities between solving computer problems and discovering alternate methods of opening a lock. You will be surprised at just how your lock pick will draw a landscape in your mind's eye as it probes the pin ridges of a lock. Unlike working with computers, lock picking is a problem solved without the aid of sight. Your only input device is a pick and tension tool, and the only sound you listen for are the clicks of the lock mechanism.

If you want to join a sport that is mentally challenging and that will allow you to compete with your peers for fun, then lock picking might be a sport for you. However, if you are only reading this book so you can learn how to become a thief, you are probably not going to learn anything in this book to help you because thieves use hammers and crowbars. And after all, if you really wanted to be a thief, you'd work for a software company.

Legal Disclaimer:

If you use any information in this book to commit a crime, you alone are responsible for your actions and should be held accountable accordingly. Think of it as though this was a book on competitive rifle sharp shooting, and someone uses the information to commit a crime using the techniques used in the book. The information and techniques in this book are for use on locks and equipment that either you own or have the expressed permission to use. I do not advocate any illegal use of the information or instruction on opening locks in this book.

Why Are "Hackers" Interested in Lock Picking?

In my opinion picking steel locks is the physical manifestation of its digital counter part, computers. Picking a lock is like solving a puzzle in much the same way it is to solve computer or networking issues, with the exception that you can physically touch a lock. As a computer professional, you develop computer skills that allow you to quickly fix problems based on experience. Picking locks presents the same challenges and taxes your memories from previous lock picking exercises. The fun of lock picking or combination cracking can very well be an occupational hazard in the daily routine of problem solving. Many computer people use the excuse of learning how to hack computers on the premise that you can't protect your network without first knowing the tricks of a hacker. You can also apply that to lock picking if you need to, I suppose. But the fact of the matter is, lock picking is a very competitive sport that is extraordinarily fun and can be extremely addictive. Much like when you were first introduced to computers, understanding how locks work is just as interesting to you as learning how computers work. I mean, if you are of that mindset.

The interest in cracking a combination lock is similar to the interest in cracking a Rubik's cube. Picking locks and cracking combinations is just another puzzle to solve, another challenge to test your brain and another way to measure yourself against your peers. Lock picking is accomplished by the manipulation of the lock by using your touch and listening to the bounce of pins and sometimes the smell of oil to the turn of the plug. There are recognizable parallels between the electronic computer realm and the real world of physical security. Finding and locating weak spots and vulnerabilities are what computer people enjoy best. So mechanical security, such as steel bolt hacking, is understandably just as interesting.

Lock Picking Sporting Groups

The creation of lock picking as a sporting group is said to have begun in Germany. What started out as a curious interest quickly grew overnight to a 500- member club, and today is around 1000 members strong. For legal reasons, and how the laws in Germany are phrased, this group of lock picking enthusiasts did not want to be classified as an organized crime group and turned their club into a lock-picking sports group. There is a very strong anti-organized crime law in Germany that essentially says if you teach someone a skill that is used to commit a crime, then you are involved in an organized crime group and will be prosecuted with the person who actually committed the crime. One could understand how 500 lock pickers assembling together and teaching each other how to pick locks could be difficult to explain if one of the members used this knowledge to commit an illegal offense.

A sports group was invented, with rules, contracts and membership cards. A signed contractual agreement stated that each member would never use his or her knowledge to commit a crime.

So there we have it, the birth of the first organized lock picking sport group in Germany that today has more than one thousand registered members. If you go to their Web site, http://www.lockpicking.org/ you will see that this sport has extended into the Netherlands, United Kingdom, and France.

The credit could go to a man named Hans (The Unicorn) van de Looy from the Netherlands who is said to have inspired the Germans.

Toool
(The Open Organisation of Lockpickers) The Netherlands

In the Netherlands, there is a group founded by Barry Wels named Toool (The Open Organization of Lockpickers) www.Toool.nl Barry told me that he is "personally proud of the fact that Toool has grown from a bunch of lock picking (computer) freaks to a well-respected organization."

Some examples of this are when Barry and his group are called upon to give expert testimony in court cases and they are frequently invited by lock companies to demonstrate lock vulnerabilities. He said that very recently they have discovered a serious flaw in a lock that allows even an untrained person access in less than 5 seconds. He also told me "Even a forensics expert wouldn't be able to detect that this lock was not opened with the proper key." They informed the company that manufactured the lock, and after they verified Toool's claim, production was stopped and all locks still in stores were recalled. Barry said that he is going to demonstrate this flaw at his up coming visit to the Hope conference in New York.

Barry also said that he and his group enjoy having lock manufacturing companies change their claims on their websites about specific locks that cannot be picked. This has happened with the Abus Plus system. Abus changed the way the lock worked, but now we have created a new tool to open the complete Abus Plus series. This new tool will also be demonstrated at the 5th Hope in New York.

Toool has also set up a new form of lock picking competition. They have selected 26 locks, where members come into the club and work on them in the evenings, through out the year. Each picking of a lock is begun with a click of a stopwatch and a 'stop' once the lock is compromised. You are allowed to tension the lock, but not insert the pick before you press start.

Barry says that the simplest lock that can be picked is number 09, brand name '909', a cheap European lock from the market. Paul Boven opened it in 0:00.75 (yes, three quarters of a second), including pressing start and stop on the stopwatch ;) Barry's best time is 0:00.97 (just under one second) But he admits that they have only recently begun this type of competition.

As a reference, here are the new times we have set to the locks in the ongoing Toool lock pick competition:

http://node-c-0696.a2000.nl/~paul/toool-strijd.html

"Of course we will still have the traditional 'Dutch Open' championship, that is open to every sport lock picker."

Barry often attends the HOPE, an annual hackers convention in New York, and gives lock picking demonstrations to all those that attend. Watching Barry is a great resource for seasoned and beginner lock pickers alike. You may contact him from his website at www.toool.nl

dc719 Crew

The dc719 crew (dc719.org) is a collection of young technology geeks who get together for discussions, projects, and social events in Colorado Springs, Colorado. Major interests lean towards information security, networking, and physical security. dc719 is the first ever DefCon Group (defcon.org), that was started by local area people who share an interest in technology and a love for all things DefCon. The group is very diverse with ages ranging from mid teens to "that's none of your business".

At Def Con 11 (2003), the dc719 crew introduced the first annual lock picking contest, LPCON. In its first year with over 40 contestants it was a huge success. So much so, that to appease the fire marshal, the contest and its crowd of onlookers was moved to an outdoor setting. Digital timing is used in order to facilitate up to six simultaneous competitors using hand made electronics and software written by the group. The first official champion was Qmark, who managed to open the final 3 locks of the competition in under 3 minutes. His toolset of choice is a set of picks ground down from old street sweeper brushes. The contest is updated yearly and will see an expansion of an added obstacle course at Def Con 12.

dc719 also provides lock boards at DefCon and their monthly meetings for people to get a chance to practice and / or strut their stuff. The sharing of information is the main goal of the group, both in teaching others and learning themselves.

For DefCon / LPCon FAQ:
http://www.worldwidewardrive.org/dclp/LPCONFAQ.html

For DefCon / LPCon Rules and Registration:
http://www.worldwidewardrive.org/dclp/DCLP.html

I first heard about this event from my friend in San Diego, Will Nett. He sent me my first lock picking set and told me that everyone he has introduced to lock picking became addicted. I just laughed at that statement. All of Will's friends are computer geeks. Still, he was right. After the first lock sprung open, I too was addicted. It must be a computer thing.

I first heard the term "pass around" on a lock picking website **www.lockpicking101.com**

Lockpicking101

Within the forums of Lockpicking101, you will find an invaluable wealth of information and sources for everything concerning lockpicking and locksmithing.

From How to's to What to buy, we discuss it all.

Looking for a place to start? Read through these threads, as they answer some of the most common questions.

http://www.lockpicking101.com/viewforum.php?f=2

The FAQ's there will answer many of the most common questions asked, such as:

- What are the rules for this site?
- What picks do I buy? Where from?
- How do I impression a key?
- Are there video guides to lock picking?
- What is the proper terminology?
- What's the Law in my province/country/state?
- Where/when can I take a course/get a license?

..and much more.

Introduce yourself, and don't forget to bookmark this site and visit often. This forum has a wide spectrum of frequent users from around the world from stark newbies to old pro's. Read the FAQ's, use the search feature to look up your questions, then post away and share your experiences with them. We look forward to meeting you soon.

A Pass Around

A pass around is when a group of lock pickers sign up to exchange locks. A pass around can be a local event or through the mail. The purpose of a pass around is to allow different pickers to explore possible exploits of someone else's lock and then share these vulnerabilities with your group. The nice thing about a pass around is there may be several different ways to pick a lock that you wouldn't otherwise be exposed to. A pass around also allows you to participate with your peers in a common hobby, share techniques and information.

Websites like, Lockpicking101.com, are a good place to meet other hobbyists. The Open Organization Of Lockpickers, (TOOOL) and Lockpicking.org are good informational sites, and Security.org is a place for the serious lock picker.

- www.lockpicking101.com
- http://www.nvhs.nl/index-eng.php
- www.security.org
- www.lockpicking.org

A Competitive Pass Around

A competitive pass around is when a group of lock pickers pass around several locks and compete against each other to see who can pick the fastest. However, you might want to set guidelines ahead of time on what types of instruments can be used so everyone uses the same picks.

You may join a pass around or start one in your area from groups on Yahoo.com or Google.com , or join www.lockpicking101.com and hook up with one there.

Performance Anxiety

Performance anxiety can cause someone who is a master lock pick in his or her living room to turn into a fumbling nervous ten-thumbed amateur. Every lock pick has a couple of locks that he or she can open without the slightest effort. But something happens between opening the lock in under 5 seconds in your living room and stabbing at it in front of real people that makes you look and feel ridiculous. It's not an uncommon phenomenon; it can strike down anyone, any time and at the exact moment you lose confidence in yourself. Confidence picks locks, and you build confidence through practice. A little trick that some people will do is to bring their easiest lock with them to a competition or demonstration. A lock that you know you can pick acts as a motivation lock. Once you pop open that lock a couple of times, you're ready to go. There's also the possibility that you get so nervous that you can't open your motivation lock. If this happens to you just tell yourself that most of the people that are likely to show up at a lock picking contest are probably little Nancy's too, and just be happy that no one towel whacks you back to your car.

I think any locksmith will tell you that it is easy to be intimidated when a customer is standing behind you making rude comments as you are trying to let them back into their house or car and you're having a difficult time picking the lock. The customer might say things like, "good thing my house isn't on fire, James Bond" or "ever pick a lock before?" Those types of comments can easily persuade a locksmith to drill out the pins and charge the wise cracking client to pay for a new lock—plus installation.

All kidding aside, anyone can suffer the affliction of performance anxiety, or the arrogance of too much confidence. I can sit down and open the same lock in under 3 seconds all night long, and it doesn't matter what type of pick I use; a diamond head pick, a rake, a paperclip, or whatever. But sometimes I will sit down with the same lock, use the same picks and can't open it at all. I call that too much confidence. Never assume you are going to open the lock. Always stick to a specific proven pattern for every style of lock you pick. It's a lot like troubleshooting a networking problem. You first try to connect to a local computer, then the router and past the router. Develop your own pattern of solving each lock that you try to pick. Many times even the same model will be slightly different because of manufacturing flaws. So always assume every lock is different and you are discovering it for the first time.

The Legality of Owning Lock Picking Tools?

In general, you will have to look up the laws for the state or providence you live in to answer this question. I don't believe it is against the law to possess or carry locking picking tools, but if you use them to commit a crime, it is most definitely a felony. I would advise you check with your local law enforcement agency. Many laws state that it is illegal to carry burglary tools on your self or in your vehicle. That is; *tools that you intend to commit acts of burglary with,* or have already done so. A hammer and crowbar can be considered a burglary tool in the right or wrong settings. Lock picking tools can be considered burglary tools. I personally don't see the necessity in having to carry any lock picking tools on my self, although I know many hobbyists like to carry a pair of wallet sized picks with them at all times. I know they can come in handy sometimes to help people that have locked themselves out of something, but that is still a weak argument if you have to explain it to a police officer. Another valid point to make is that most computer people aren't typically in a situation where the police are searching them either.

3 Time Redundant Disclaimer:

As far as I know, the computer people that have participated it lock picking are doing it in a legal manner and are in no way using their knowledge of lock picking to break into people's homes or personal property. This book is only to be used as a guide to help learn lock picking as a sport and possible platform into a career of being a locksmith. The author of this book does not advocate breaking any laws and cannot be held accountable for anyone that misuses the information stored in these texts. If anyone uses the knowledge that I provide in this book in any illegal activity to my knowledge, I will have no choice but to report you to the authorities. In other words, don't brag to me in e-mail about the use of this book illegally or e-mail me asking how to break into someone's personal property.

A Word About Locksmiths

I'm not sure if Locksmithing can be considered an ancient trade, or if it's even an actual word, but it certainly is a very old craft. Steel locks date back thousands of years as do locksmiths. I believe there are two ways to become a locksmith; you can attend a locksmith school, or be hired as an apprentice. Either way you are going to have to start at the bottom and learn your way up. Locksmiths pass their knowledge down from apprentice to pupil in a very discrete and very secretive fashion. This book isn't going to teach anyone to become a locksmith. Locksmiths spend more time installing or re-keying locks than they do picking them. Not all locksmiths are great lock pickers just like not all computer people are programmers. However, this book does teach some basic fundamentals that locksmith's use, but some of the phrases and terms may not be exact as I am not a locksmith, just a computer geek and lock-picking enthusiast.

As I said earlier, the trend of computer hackers that are interested in lock picking (and I use the word hacker loosely to describe all computer people) is spreading quickly among computer professionals, and some not so professional. The techniques taught in this book are for legal and lawful lock picking as a hobby, and used to help a novice that is interested in learning lock picking as a hobby and for hackers that are considering entering lock picking competitions in such events as in Defcon.

Note: For those of you that don't know, Defcon is the largest underground hacking event in the world. There is computer hacking and lock picking competitions, among other events.

"Picking locks is easy." Lock picking is nothing more than utilizing a locks mechanical defect, (or in many cases, defects, as there is usually more than one defect in a lock) and exploiting them. Most picking concepts are basic and are easily applied to most locks. A good lock picker knows where defeats will resist within a lock based on experience and from studying the inside of a lock. It's just like computers, you can't exploit security holes without first taking the time to learn how data is passed through the different network layers. Locksmiths know how to pick locks because they know what the inside of a lock looks like and how all the parts work together.

The "Key" to Lock Picking

"Know the lock, be at one with the lock."

-- Weird guy that spoke to me in the mall.

Serious lock pickers own more than one lock of the same type - one lock for picking and one for taking apart. I have a box full of disassembled locks. To reverse-engineer a lock you must cut it open. There are several kinds of tools that you can use to cut open a steel lock case with, and many can be very expensive. To keep it cheap all you really need is an inexpensive rotary tool, like a Dremel, A cheap workshop vise to hold it steady, and small cut-away disks. Below is a list of tools that I use.

- Workshop Vise – $12
- Dremel rotary tool – $50
- Dremel cut off wheels – $12
- Eye goggles – $2
- Broken Dremel disk in my eye…priceless

Note: Some people own a grinding wheel to make their own picking tools. Grinding wheels start at $40.

Figure1.1 Vise and Tool

In *Figure* 1.1 you will see where I bound a padlock to a steel vise and used the Dremel and a cut-off pad. The first thing that I did was to cut off the six metal pin taps from the bottom of the lock, and then I used a hammer and screwdriver to separate it. However, sometimes you can just take a screwdriver and wedge it off. In the example on the same picture, I had to take the Dremel tool and cut along the underside of the plate, cutting through a plastic bumper. With a small screwdriver I then pried off the bottom plate of the padlock.

As you will see in *Figure 1.2*, what remains is a spring for the shackle, and the plug (some people call the plug a tumbler). The top of the plug is where the bottom pins and springs are; the large spring is for the shackle, (a shackle is the steel U that locks in place) and the cut away base. When the plug is turned it turns a latch at the top inside of the lock case and springs open the shackle. Some padlocks you can simply run your pick to the top on the inside and push the latch aside, or can just use padlock shims to slide down beside the shackle and turn. Both methods I will go over in later chapters.

1.2 Cut Padlock

Once you are familiar with the inter-mechanisms of a lock and how all the moving parts work together, you will have a mental image to map your progress while picking a lock. Because every lock manufacturer builds a lock differently, you will want to cut open and examine as many locks as you can. I think you will find though, that after four or five cheap locks you will become easily bored and will want to move up to the more expensive locks that have built in security.

Note: As with many hobbies, collecting locks can become an expensive habit. To help offset these cost, you can ask all of your friends and families if they have any old locks that they've lost the keys to or simply don't use anymore. Most people will keep old unused locks with no keys because they think one day they'll find the key and wished they had not thrown the lock away. You will be surprised by how many you can collect this way.

To compete in lock picking contest with your peers, or to even become a "Master Lock Picker," you will have to know how to break into numerous locks. With experience you will earn the skills to explore new locks for the first time and immediately be able to exploit what you find. And believe me, once you realize just how easy it is to pick a lock, you won't sleep at night until you rework your own home security system.

A Word About Car Locks

Purposely I chose not to include a section about opening car doors and car ignitions. The purpose of this book is to help prepare readers who are interested learning lock picking as a hobby or considering entering a lock picking competition, not how to become a car thief. There are many hobbyists that use their knowledge to help people that are locked out of their car, in fact more people lock themselves out of their cars than their houses, but still I feel that picking car locks is out of the scope of this book.

How Many Locks Should I Purchase to Practice With

Everyone has his or her limit on just how many locks is too many. A good indicator that you have too many locks happens when you begin hiding them from your spouse because you don't want to hear about it again. This may also apply to roommates, parents, life partners and small children concerned about their college fund. Once you pick your first couple of locks, you will find yourself driving down the road and after spotting a hardware store, swinging in to see what kind of locks they have. I myself have taken a lunch break or two in a hardware store to find a lock I've never picked before. I purchased it, sat in my car and picked it open and felt stupid for wasting $15 or more.

"Picking locks is easy." You use your touch more than your vision, and your hearing for the clicks. I know in the beginning it might not seem so easy - your hands might cramp up around a lock pick after an hour of unsuccessfully trying to open it. You might curse the lock, curse me for saying how easy it is and curse yourself for being too stupid to figure it out. The first lock that I bought I quickly opened and threw away the package that read "Lock Pick Resistance" I struggled a week with that lock and even broke a pick off inside it. Completely and utterly frustrated, I stomped over to the hardware store and bought 5 more locks. That night while watching the National Geographic channel, I began again. To my surprise I opened the first lock immediately, and then two more in under 5 minutes. On the 3rd lock I even discovered that if I poked around towards the top, I could push a latch that opened the padlock without picking the pins. The two other locks that I purchased I picked the next day, and one of them was a pick resistant lock like the first one that I had trouble with.

I would recommend that you start with a couple of cheap padlocks and work your way up from there. Easy locks will help you build confidence and dexterity for more difficult locks to pick. Once you master picking padlocks you can work your way to combination padlocks, deadbolts and even push button combination door locks.

For me, lock picking allows me to solve a physical puzzle, one that relies more on touch than it does digital programming errors, like working with computer networks and server buffer overflows. And locks don't have the advantage of being able to download a program patch once a flaw is discovered. So if I haven't made lock picking sound fun yet, then keep reading because I'm going to explain how to use picking techniques and methods that will open almost every locked door that you may encounter. If you like discovering new ways to hack computers, you're going to love learning about lock picking. One of the best things about writing this book for me is, unlike my website, TheNetworkAdministrator.com when I explain the latest hacking tips and tricks, I don't have to worry about you breaking into my web server…just my house. I don't know if I like that any better.

What Tools Should I Begin With?

For the beginner I recommend just a cheap basic lock picking set for under $20.00. Some people become frustrated in the beginning because they didn't pick the lock immediately and quit. You don't want to be too heavily invested in tools if you are the type to quit. Although, I should say that most computer people don't give up easy and are typically in it for the learning curve.

There are several places on the Internet to purchase lock picks:

http://www.thenetworkadministrator.com/lockpicks.htm
http://www.lockpicks.com/
http://www.selfdefenseproducts.com/lockpick.htm.
http://www.force-ten.com/locks1.html
http://www.lockpicktools.net/?looksmart

The Tools of a Lock Picker

There are two main tools used to pick a key lock, and those are the Pick and the Torque Wrench. The pick is used to press driver keys and the torque wrench is used to apply pressure on the plug. You may use any device that is thin enough and strong enough to push a key top pin and turn the plug. However, there are pre-made instruments that you can purchase that will make it a little easier on a beginner. Maybe later you will be confident enough or just plain bored enough, that you will use a paper clip too. Still, lock picking involves more than just tools, it's being able to use your touch and feel in conjunction with what ever instrument you use, because if you can't feel the click of the pins and master your senses, you're not going to be able to be a master lock picker.

Next, let's look at some basic lock picking tools.

Basic Lock Picking Tools

In Figure 1.3 you will see 10 of the most common types of picks used. Listed below that picture you will find their corresponding names.

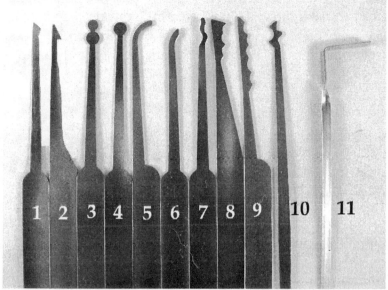

Figure 1.3 shows the Lock Pick Set that I use.

1. Large Diamond Pick
2. Broken Key Extractor
3. Double-ball Pick
4. Single-ball Pick
5. Long Hook Pick
6. Short Hook Pick
7. C Rake Hook
8. Wafer Pick
9. L Rake Pick
10. S Rake Pick
11. W Twist-flex Torque Wrench

Some people like to use dental picks. The dental picks in *Figure* 1.5 are a set of 5 that I found on the Internet for less than $4.95 a set. These tools are not actually dental picks, although I have real dental picks as well, they are only called dental picks and are typically used for crafts. Some, like the picks shown below, are a little thicker than a locks key way and have to be filed down. On high security locks, you sometimes need to reach around a high pin to tap a smaller hidden one.

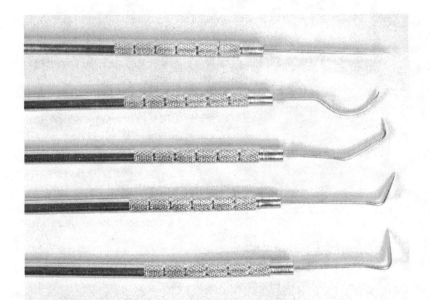

Figure 1.4 shows a set of dental picks.

 My favorite pick is a paperclip. I can bend the tip anyway I want, use one to pick and another as a tension tool. And most of all, I don't have to worry whether or not it is legal to carry them on me.

Pick Guns and Electronic Pickers

There are also such tools as lock picking guns. Before the plug of the lock-and-turn, the shear line must be free of pins. A pick gun or an electronic picker will snap or vibrate the pins past the shear line while you apply torque on the plug. Locksmiths will use a pick gun or a vibrating picker, but a locksmith is providing a service to his customer the fastest way possible to him. Most computer people that are into lock picking as a hobby or sport wouldn't typically use a lock-picking gun because it might be considered cheating. Personally I don't use the pick gun that I have, it was purely an impulse purchase and I like the challenge of picking a lock by hand. Still, the lock-picking gun can come in handy if you are helping someone that is locked out of his or her house and the lock is a difficult one to pick by hand.

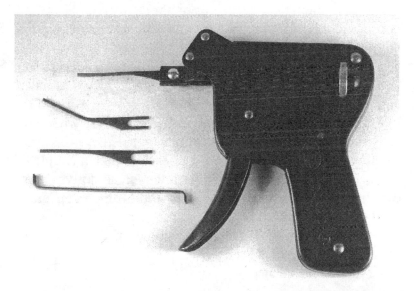

Figure 1.5 Lock Picking Gun that is used to vibrate the pins up.

Making Your Own Tools?

There are a lot of locksmith professionals and hobbyists that like to make their own tools. They have wheel grinders and other types of metal grinding tools. Some like to fabricate their tools from steak knifes, spring steel, hacksaw blades, bicycle spokes and I've even heard where people use the metal from a plumbers snake. If you're the type that likes a difficult challenge, you can start out with two paperclips. For the rest of you though, I would just recommend spending the twenty bucks.

A Word Concerning Lock Picking Tools

It should be said that it is not the tools that make the picker. In other words, you don't need a set of elaborate custom crafted lock picking tools to become a good lock picker. Many seasoned lock picks make their own tools out of household items. Some prefer only to use paperclips and hairpins and believe if you can't pick with a paper clip, you're not a picker. Once you become a good lock picker you can use anything that you would like and have as much opinion on what other people are doing wrong as you'd like. In fact, there will be plenty of time for that when you become a senior citizen. But until you get there, take my simple advice in this book and lets learn to pick a couple of locks before we start grinding down steak knives, and twisting lock picks from piano wire and all the other picks used by the gung-ho.

Once you get the feel for picking a lock, and understand the mechanics behind it, what tools you use will be of little consequence.

Holding Your Picks

The most common way used to hold a lock pick is like you would hold a pencil. It's a little awkward at first, but you want to develop good lock picking habits in the beginning. This method of holding picks allows just the right pressure without being too excessive and bending or breaking your picks. If you can't push the pins holding a pick like this, than you are exerting too much pressure with your turning tool.

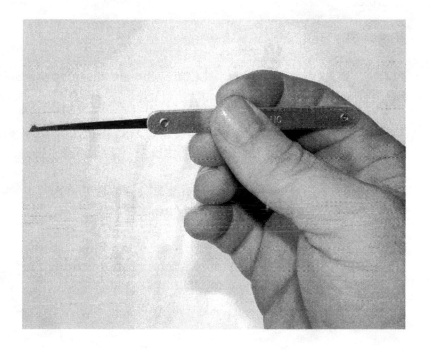

"Don't fall asleep on me yet, we are almost there…"

Basics Terms

Here are some quick basic terms about a lock that you should know:

Plug: The plug is the unit on the lock that holds the bottom pins and turns to open. The plug is also the unit on the lock that the key slides into.

Key way: The Key way is the slot in which the key is inserted.

Hull: The Hull holds the pins and springs.

Bottom Pins: (or Key pins) Bottom pins are the pins that touch the key when it is inserted

Top Pins: (or Set Pins) are the pins that are pushed up into the hull, past the shear line by the bottom pins.

Pin Springs: Pin springs are the metal springs that sit on top of the drive pins and exert a downward force.

Shear Line: The Shear Line is between the Plug and the Hull. When all the top pins, or drive pins, are lined up, the plug is allowed to rotate and the lock will open.

The Anatomy of a Lock

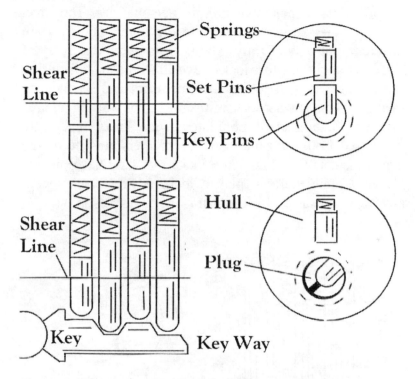

Figure 1.6 shows the plug face on and in a cross section

As you can see from *Figure1*.6 the ridges of the key line up the top pins so there are no overlapping pins in the way of the shear line. This means that the plug is free to turn. The pin and tumbler model of locks is the most common lock used. It is in padlocks, deadbolts and door handles. The concept for picking this type of lock is easy. Simply set the bottom pins beyond the shear line, like a key would do, while applying pressure using your turning tool or torque wrench. Once all the top pins are clear the plug is free to turn.

Lock Characteristics

All locks have their own unique personalities. They feel different, they react differently to the touch, and they are different, but only slightly. The trick is in the discovery of just how slightly. Most locks have inherent manufacturing flaws and it is your job to find them out and set them to memory. This is what locksmiths do - they work in an area that is predominately populated with locks that were purchased from the same hardware dealers, and he or she over time sets to memory the locks that they have picked. Never assume you can pick a lock. A good lock picker always approaches a lock as if it is his or her first time.

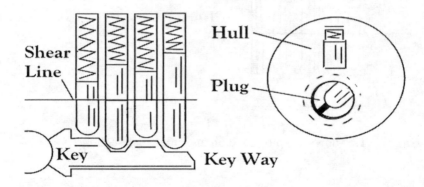

Figure 1.7 shows how the bottom pins line up when a key is inserted.

You are as good as the locks that you have mastered. Before we try picking our first lock, let's take a look at how a key opens one. From the picture in *Figure* 1.7 you can see that when the key is inserted into the plug, the pins are perfectly aligned to allow a line between the bottom pins and the top pins. This line is known as the shear line. When the bottom pins are lined up at the shear line, the plug can be turned. When picking a lock, you are trying to place the top pins above the shear line.

As you can see from the picture illustrated in *Figure*1.7, the bottom pins (or bottom pins) are different in size than the top pins, almost like a code. The code is cracked when the correct key is inserted. I realize that you already know this, and are probably getting bored and want to get to the good stuff, but I want you to maintain a strong mental image of how a lock and key works. It is this mental imaging that will help you pick a lock. If you can visualize what you are doing using touch and the click of the pins, then your brain can draw a picture and track your work. Knowing what the inside of a lock looks like and how the key interacts with it will make you a much better lock picker.

"Stay with me, we're almost there…"

Hand Warm-ups

Doing hand warm-ups is a good practice to get into before picking a lock, whether you are a beginner or professional. (I don't mean professional like a thief). As you are starting out, your fingers will become easily tired. This is mainly attributed to the fact that you are using muscles that you haven't typically used before. Even if you're like me and are a strong typist on the computer keyboard, your fingers will tire and cramp when you first use the pick and torque wrench.

To warm up, gently stretch your fingers back and forth, bend your knuckles and possibly bring your hands together flat and press your fingers back and forth like finger pushups. Picking a lock can be very demanding on virgin hands and fingers, so until you can build up come dexterity, you might want to start slow.

Locksmith's Tips on Picking Locks

If you are working with older locks, here are a few tips that locksmiths use when picking pin tumbler locks.

1. Lubricate the plug with WD40 or any other spray. Do NOT use graphite. Use your raking pick to distribute the lubricant across the pins. Most locks have been exposed to weather and can have grit and dust inside clinging to the pins.

2. If you are helping someone, ask questions. Sometimes the person you are helping will reveal that the key hasn't worked for a while. This could mean something is stuck inside or the lock has simply failed. Don't give up though; you may still be able to pick the lock.

3. Ask which direction the key turns. Sometimes a lock won't open because you assume the key turns in the wrong direction. Kwickset locks for example always pick to the left to unlock. This is the opposite direction to most brands. Other locks such as Schlage have models that pick in either direction.

4. Use the tension tool that fits the keyway closely. Always begin with little tension. Most pins don't need a lot of pressure to bind in the shear line. Rake the pins first and

then try pressing on them. Too much torque on your tension wrench can make your job more difficult. If the keyway is too small for your tension wrench, try bending and using a small paper clip.

And always have a paperclip and hairpin among your tools. You never know when one will come in handy.

Selecting Our First Lock to Pick

The first lock that we will select to pick is a padlock because they are easier to hold for our first experience with lock picking. If you don't already have a lock, you will need to purchase one.

<u>Purchasing a Lock:</u>

I'm going to restate choosing a cheap lock for your first lock to pick. Go to any hardware store, or any store that sells padlocks and look for an inexpensive pin tumbler padlock. I wouldn't really consider Master Lock as a cheap lock, but in my area, Master Lock is the main lock sold. If this is the case in your area, get a Master Lock No.1. That's a good first lock to learn on. Cheaper locks are easier to pick, and it is a good launching platform to more difficult locks. Also a cheap lock has multiple vulnerabilities. You can pick them with a pick, use your pick to depress the unlocking levels locked at the top of the inside of the lock, and padlock shims fit and turn easier.

Warning: Be careful not to purchase a warded padlock for your first lock by mistake. A warded padlock is similar to a skeleton key and uses a completely different method of picking that is discussed in later chapters.

Figure 1.8 is a warded lock and key.

Holding the padlock

Hold your padlock with the pins at the top of the key way. Some people will hold the lock upside down because it feels easier on their fingers. If you hold the lock upside down, gravity can cause the bottom pins to fall back into the shear line. Holding the lock upright allows the pins to fall away from the shear line. It also allows you to differentiate the feel of the pins that are pressed down upon by the top springs, or fall freely with gravity. It is still possible to pick a lock upside down, (I am told that most of the locks in Europe are installed upside down) it is just a little more difficult to do.

If you notice in *Figure* 1.9, I hold the padlock in one hand, and also push down on the torque wrench with the fingers from the same hand. This frees up my other hand to pick the lock. If this is uncomfortable for you, then simply play around with it until you find a position that works best for you. Left-handed people would simply use their right hand to hold the lock and their left to pick with.

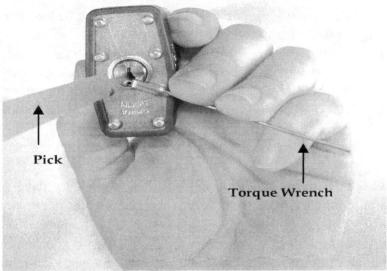

Figure 1.9 Holding a padlock

Counting the Pins

The first thing that I like to do is count how many pins I'm going to be working with. Typically in a padlock there are only 4 pins, sometimes more on expensive locks. I always begin with my half-diamond pick and will drag it on the roof of the plug and count the pins. Because there is little or nothing you can actually see without the aid of a scope, you must rely on feel to count your pins. As I drag my pick along the top of the pins, I can feel that some pins are a little bouncier than others. Once a pin is set in its corresponding hull, you will feel that it has lost its bounce from the spring above the top, or set, pin.

Which Direction Does the Plug Turn

The torque wrench is the tool that you will use to turn the plug. Most padlocks may turn in either direction. Sometimes if you are unsure you can insert your torque wrench and turn it in both directions. One direction will have a very stiff, solid feeling "stop" when torque is applied. This is NOT the direction to turn. The other direction will have a fairly "mushy" stop, which is the opening direction.

Now that we are ready to pick our lock I want to make a final comment: You must exercise patience. Not everyone will get it on the first few attempts; it takes some people days before they successfully open a lock. It's easy to become frustrated and give up, when this happens, simply walk away and try again later. Only practice combined with diligence will make you a good lock picker. This is why lock picking isn't for criminals. Someone wanting to use the information in this book to help commit a crime would never read this many pages before committing a crime. That's why most burglars use a hammer and crowbar.

> **Lock Picking Facts**:
> In spy movies when you see the hero walk up to a door and insert a single pick and he or she immediately opens the door, that tool is called a key.

Picking a Padlock

Now we're ready to begin. Insert the torque wrench into the base of the keyway, (or to an area that will not obstruct you from entering your pick) and gently apply pressure to the turn. The purpose of this is to bind a top pin in the shear line. The pressure from your torque wrench will immediately bind one pin, sometimes two. With your pick, you can easily feel your way to the bound pin because it is the one with the greatest resistance. *Figure* 1.10 shows how pins are bound when the plug is turned.

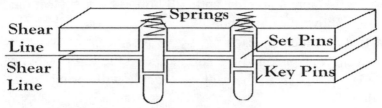

Figure 1.10 shows the first pin being bound when torque is put on the base of the key way.

Once this has occurred you can push the bound pin clear of the shear line and up into the hull of the lock. With the first pin up and out of the way of the shear line, you will feel the plug turn slightly until the next binding pin stops it again.

The next step is to push the next pin up and out of the way. *Figure* 1.11 shows the first pin clear and how the plug immediately binds the next pin. The next pin to bind isn't necessarily the next in the role. It may depend on thickness, spring tension or height.

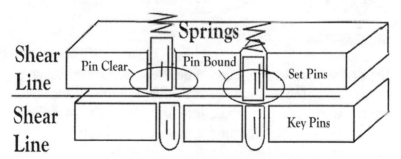

Figure 1.11 shows the first top pin clearing the shear line, leaving the next top pin bound and ready to be pushed in.

As you can see from *Figure* 1.11, the first top pin has been pushed up past the shear line that was binding it.

With one pin clear, the plug moved a little more in the direction of the tension and traps the next pin above the shear line. With your pick you push up the next pin and then all remaining pins until all top pins are clear and seated above the shear line. With practice you will be able to feel and identify each pin by its resistance between the push of your pick and the spring above the top pin. When the last pin is clear, the padlock shackle will spring up and unlock.

Figure 1.12 shows a successfully picked lock

Just to recap:

One of the best ways to determine the greatest resistance to the pins is by touch. Insert your torque wrench, or whatever turning tools you are using into the key way of a lock. Apply and maintain turning pressure on the plug, while using your picking tool to gently move each of the pins one at a time. The tumbler that is the most difficult to move has the greatest resistance. This tumbler is picked first.

Once the first pin is picked, the plug will rotate slightly. While maintaining turning pressure on the plug, the next pin or two will become wedged against the shear line. As each pin is picked, the plug will turn until the lock is sprung open. Just remember not to release the turning pressure on the plug, otherwise all the pins will fall back into the shear line and you will have to begin again.

Different Picking Methods:

There are three types of picking methods generally used to pick a lock: Pin Pressing, Bouncing and Scrubbing (some people also refer to Scrubbing as Raking).

- Pin pressing is when you use a diamond tipped pick and gently push the pins up past the shear line and into the hull.
- Scrubbing or raking is when you use a rake pick and run it really quickly back and forth against the pins.
- Bouncing is when you insert your pick into the keyway and gently rock the tip of your tool up and down and you move back and forth against the pins, while applying minimal tension using your torque wrench.

Remember that the purpose of your torque wrench is to bind a pin in the shear line so you can push it into its slot. If you pull back and do not maintain constant pressure, the pins that you've successfully pushed into place will fall back down past the shear line and you will have to start over again. Executed correctly with the right amount of torque and by correctly pushing in your pins, you will be successful.

How Much Pressure Should I Use With the Torque Wrench?

When using the torque wrench it's important not to put so much force on the wrench that it traps the pins and makes them impossible to push in. At the same time you also don't want to put so little pressure on the turn that the pins pop back out again. While practicing, you will find just the right amount of pressure to make it work.

I did everything that you instructed, and it didn't work?

If you haven't successfully picked a lock on your first try, don't be disappointed. Quite frankly I would have been surprised if you did. It takes time and a lot of patience to pick your first lock. Even when you did everything I instructed and the lock still didn't open, it's all right - don't become frustrated with it. Give your fingers a rest, (they are a little sore, aren't they) and continue reading on. If you have successfully picked your first lock, that's great. But there are still a lot of pages left in this book to read.

When I pick a lock, I will first use a diamond head and press the pins in place and if that doesn't work I will take the rake or scrub the pins with a rake pick. If that doesn't work, I'll go back to the diamond pick and bounce the pins. So it's not uncommon to use all three methods while picking a lock. Although, I find that if I don't have it open with the first 3 or 4 minutes I sometimes become frustrated and will stop and give it a rest. The problem with starting over is the moment that you let go of the torque wrench you will hear all four pins snap back down. Then you ask yourself, did I just hear 3 pins or 4? Maybe there are 5 pins on this lock and I only got 4? So you try it again with the exact same results; it feels like all the pins are up, there doesn't seem to be anything left to push in? So you let go and hear the pins snap back out again. If this is what you experience, then when you get to this point, try experimenting with different pick types. Remember that paperclip I spoke of in earlier chapters? Try using it. Open up the paperclip and put a bend on the end.

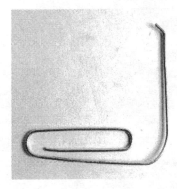

With that in mind, let's explore the anatomy of a pin tumbler padlock.

Anatomy of a Pin Tumbler Padlock

The best way to pick a lock is to know what it looks like on the inside. Before we can even think about trying to pick our first lock, lets take a look at its guts.

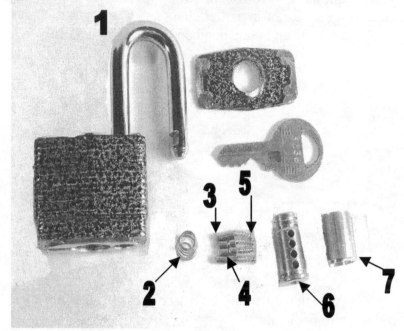

Figure 1.13 shows parts of a padlock

1. Steel Shackle in a locked position is held in place by a latch that is not shown in Figure 1.13. The locking latch is wedged between the two grooves located on the shackle.
2. The shackle spring gives the shackle its lift when the latch is released.
3. Bottom pins are the pins that touch the key and are used to adjust the height of the top pins, (or top pins) above the shear line.
4. Top pins are the pins that must be set above the shear line so the plug can turn the lever to open the lock.

5. Pin springs are the springs that keep the opposing force on the top pins and pushing them into the shear line so a lock cannot open.

6. The **P**lug is the section of the lock that houses both the bottom pins and the top pins when the lock is engaged.

7. The **H**ull is the section of the tumbler that encases the pull. The upper section of the hull is where the top pins reside when the lock is engaged to be open.

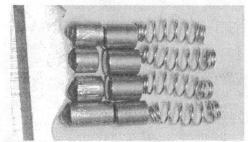

Picture of key, bottom pins, top pins and springs

Padlock Shims

Another method of opening a padlock is using padlock shims. Padlock shims are thinly formed stiff metal designed to slide between the shafts of a shackle on the toe or heel or even both. When the padlock shim is turned, it can block the latch from entering the shackle lock groove. Using padlock shims is often a faster and easier way to open a padlock. Padlock shims work on 90 percent of the most common padlocks and are typically faster at opening the lock than picking. Shims do require practice with different styles of locks, as the shackle lever is located in different positions. But even with a foreign padlock you can usually feel your way around and open one.

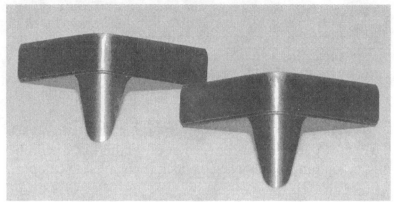

Figure 1.14 shows 2 Padlock Shims

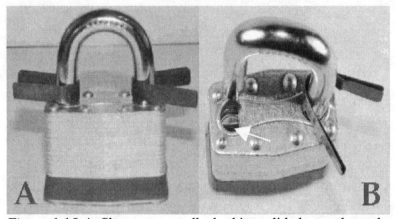

Figure 1.15-A Shows two padlock shims slid down along the shackle and blocking the lock latch from inserting into grooves on the shackle. 1.15-B shows the same lock opened with shims and an arrow pointing to the latch lever inside.

Padlock shims work on most padlocks, and generally come in four sizes. You can find them on the Internet for around $20 a set. When using a padlock shim you have to be careful with certain locks on how you place them because one wing handle should be placed on the inside of the shackle so when you turn them, one side of the shim doesn't get caught up on the shackle. You'll know what this means when you open your first lock.

The latch in *Figure* 1.15B is to the side. With other padlocks, on which I've used this technique, the latch is usually on the inside of the hole. When you slide the shim along side the shackle and follow it into the hole, you can turn the shim and usually feel where the latch is because your shim will fit lower in some areas than others. Like with a pick, you must feel your way around to find the lowest point and then turn into the latch. *Figure* 1.15A shows two padlock shims, but some padlocks may only need one. Just listen for the clicks and any movement you can feel as you're turning the shim. Just a word of warning though, padlock shims are a little tough on the fingers. You have to gently slide the shims into place without bending them and bring the two wings together and twist hard.

Anti-Lock Picking Tricks

Even though this book is really intended to be a guide for the beginner lock-picking enthusiast, I will briefly show you some more advanced locks and picking techniques for when you become bored with the basics. Many higher-end lock makers will try to incorporate as much trickery in the tooling of a lock as they can without having to put too much money into it. Cheap locks are the easiest locks to pick. Cheap locks are the least expensive to make and have the least amount of security built into them. It's not because lock makers want their product to be easily compromised, it's because more cheap locks are sold than expensive locks, and if a lock maker adds five cents worth of effort per lock, and they sell one million cheap locks a year, they can stand to lose a lot of money. People want good security locks, but they don't really want to pay for them. So people will purchase the cheapest lock on the shelf without giving it any further thought. You too have probably purchased the cheapest lock off the shelf thinking that it was safe. The affordable variety of locks, (cheap locks) are no protection against even a beginner lock picker. Believe me, after I teach you how to pick locks, you will never again look at a padlock or even a deadbolt the same way again.

Spool Pins and Mushroom Pins

Using spool and mushroom pins in higher-end locks is one of the tricks that lock maker's employ to make their locks a little more difficult to pick. As there is no such thing as a 'pickproof' lock, (although many lock companies have temporarily crowned some of their locks as being 'pickproof' but were quickly proven wrong by a lock pick hobbyist and in turn forced to re-label them) it isn't to say that there aren't a lot of challenges when it comes to higher end security locks. Security pins, such as the types shown in *Figure* 1.16, have been engineered to prevent criminals from opening certain locks. If you look at some of the shapes, you will see that security pins are lathed down into the shapes that resemble spools and mushrooms. These types of pins are affective in jamming themselves in the shear line when the pressure of a torque wrench is used. When a spool or mushroom pin becomes bound in the shear line, it gives the picker a false sense of success when in fact the plug isn't going anywhere. Tactics like these make lock picking more challenging for hobbyists, but with time, patience and a little ingenuity any lock can be picked.

The pins shown below are high security pins that have been fabricated to prevent picking. From the top left and across, these pins are. 1. *Medeco bottom pin*, 2. *Spool pin.*, 3. *Medeco mushroom pin*, 4. *Serrated pin,* 5. *American pin*, 6. *Schlage bottom pin. (Note that this is not a security pin)*

1.   2.   3.

4.   5.   6

As you can see each pin is designed to stop how conventional pin-binding is used to pick a lock. There is one tool that is used to overcome this issue, and that is a feather spring torque wrench, shown below. This spring device gently binds the pins while you push them into place. You will still need to use a turning tool to turn the plug, as the spring wrench is only for setting it.

One way to overcome the use of security pins is the use of a *spring tension wrench*. A spring tension wrench will allow you to bounce these oddly-shaped pins past the shear line. Once the pins are freed, a standard tension wrench must be used to turn the plug. As you can see, locks that employ these measures are not impenetrable; they merely require a higher level of sophistication to pick.

One of the more famous mushroom pin locks is from the West German-made Diskus Padlock from the Abus Lock Company. This lock has a stainless steel case with only four pins and a small corrugated keyway. The cylinder on these types of diskus padlocks (Master Lock also has a diskus like padlock No. 40) are mounted upside down and has a tight keyway with four tiny mushroom cut pins. Don't allow yourself to be intimidated with this lock. I let it intimidate me and didn't think I could open it, but I did, on my first try in less than two minutes. I was so impressed with myself that I immediately ran in and showed my wife...she wasn't as impressed. I'm considering writing my next book about nerdy little things that your spouse will never care about.

Figure 1.16 Diskus Shaped Padlock

Medeco Locks

Medeco Lock Company is a maker of higher security locks that are typically used for businesses. Medeco employs the trickery of an *angular pin* design. (As seen on page 41) The difficultiy6 in picking this type of lock is that the pins are cut on an angle making it difficult to push them to their proper shear points. Additionally, they turn or twist in order to clear the cylinder-shell line. And with the added security of a very narrow key way, picking these types of locks requires thinner special tools. Some locksmiths simply cut and grind their own tools for this by making a small wedge at the top of their pick so they can twist the pick until it makes contact with the pins. Nothing is untouchable. It's a lot like trying to protect your computer network with the newest and most "secure" firewall. If someone wrote the program, then someone else can find his or her way around it. Locks are exactly the same.

Note: When picking a high security lock, sometimes you will discover a situation where one pin is much higher than another, and the high pin is not allowing you to set the smaller pin beside it. You must reach over the high pin with a thin hook like tool and set the small pin first. Some people will use a shaved down paper clip, or a # 6 wire. I use a dental pick. It's actually a lot easier to do than is sounds.

Narrow Key wards

Key wards guide the key as it enters the lock. Some key wards are too close to the pins, and can block the use of a pick. To help over come this you will have to file down a hook pick, or simply use the old stand-by paper clip. Some people even have several sized piano wires that they will use for picking.

Double sets of pins

Some locks, like Schlage locks, have two sets of top pins. (Or top pins as they are sometimes called) The second set of pins consists of master pins. This type of lock allows for two different keys. The second key is the master key. For double top pins to work, there must be a separate shear line for each key, as shown in *Figure* 1.18. Don't be too intimidated by this lock either. My view is that with two shear lines you have double the chance of picking the lock. Some of you may not be as optimistic and see two shear lines as double the chance of failure--Stop it! You must have a positive attitude to successfully pick a lock.

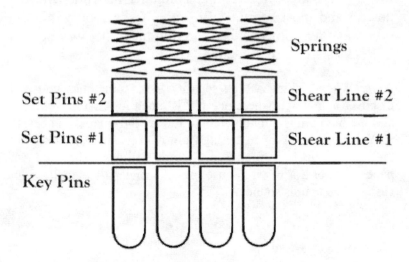

Figure 1.18 shows double top pins and dual shear lines

It's true that double top pins can make picking a lock a little challenging, but still it's not impossible. This design is intended for the master key, not to deter lock pickers.

A Warded Padlock

Warded locks may very well be the first lock design. They differ greatly from pin tumbler locks, as there are no pins to pick. A warded lock is a lot like the old lock-and-skeleton key design and they date back into the Roman and Egyptian era. The only reason I am addressing such an ancient lock is because there are still a lot of them in use today. In fact, most handcuffs use a style of ward locks. Warded padlocks are mainly used outdoors or in industrial areas were there is a lot of dirt and grime that would clog up a pin tumbler. Warded locks use levers that turn in and out of the latch zone much the same what a skeleton key would turn a lock open. The wards on the key turn the mechanism that releases the latch that holds the shackle down. In *Figure* 1.19, you see a warded padlock and two keys.

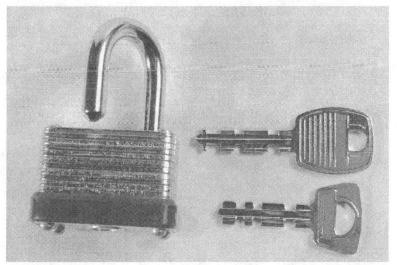

Figure 1.19 shows a warded padlock with two different keys.

The construction of a Warded lock consists of "wards" or protrusions in the lock itself. This is of course the most basic of lock-and-key systems but can also be difficult to pick if you are not familiar with them. The protrusions on the key catch the wards inside the lock and allow the mechanism to be opened. Each keyhole is designed to be manufacturer specific and carries its own unique shape. If you consider what a blank key might look like, it could be just a small square flat piece of metal. Then cuts might be made to the square piece of metal that match up to the groves inside the door mechanism.

Simply put, in a warded lock you have several cuts made in the key. These cuts are made to circumvent the wards of the lock, and ultimately open the bolt. If the cuts on the key do not match that of the internal warding, the key is shunted, and therefore cannot turn. This is how the warded lock derives its security. In *Figure* 1.20A you will see a warded padlock disassembled in its many pieces.

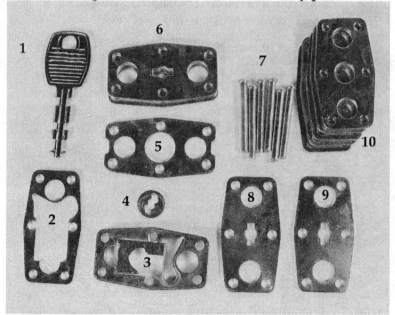

Figure 1.20A shows a warded padlock disassembled

1. Slotted Key
2. Lever Support Plate

3. Release Mechanism
4. Key Guide
5. Guide Support Plate
6. Slot Plate
7. Pins that hold plates together
8. Slot Plate
9. Slot Plate
10. Shackle Plates

Picking a Warded Lock

Like pin tumbler lock picks, there are also tools to pick warded locks. But before we look at picking a warded lock, let's first look at how the shackle is held in place. As you can see from *Figure* 1.20A, the release mechanism (#3) is the lever that holds the shackle in place. In *Figure* 1.20B you can see how the shackle is held in place.

Figure 1.20B shows how the shackle is held in place by the locking mechanism to the right of the picture.

If you look closely, #4 the spring pushes over the lever #2 the sets inside the shackle groove #1. To release the lever and open the lock, the tip of the key #3 must turn and push the lever towards the spring #4, freeing the shackle groove from the lever so the lock can open. If you just take the time to examine the picture you can work out the mechanics of it for yourself. You will have a much deeper understanding if you purchase a couple of warded locks and cut off the pins on the bottom and examine one first hand. You will learn more from reverse engineering a lock than any book can teach you.

If you examine the warded lock picks in *Figure* 1.21, you will see that unlike the keys, there are only wards on the tip of the picks. This is because only the tip of the key is needed to push aside the lever to release the shackle. Warded lock picks are designed to slide in the key way with only one protrusion at the top that turns and pushes the latch aside. The rest of the protrusion on a warded key is merely a distraction. The warded lock picking set below is the very basic set to start out with.

Figure 1.21 shows five warded lock picks

Cracking a Combination Padlock

In this next section I will show you two different ways to open a combination padlock without first knowing the combination code. This first method can be used to uncover a lost combination code and is 90 percent accurate on all Master Lock combination padlocks. I say only 90 percent because I've heard that some people say it won't work on

some locks. However, I've had a 100 percent success rate so far. Master Lock Company is said to have redesigned its 1500 series combination lock, (this is the standard combination lock that you used in school as a

child) and it showed up on the shelves somewhere in the middle of 1999 and 2000. The methods that are listed in the book may not work on those redesigned models. However, I have recently purchased three newer "1500 Series" padlocks and cracked all three. Some feel that Master Lock returned to their old design. The newer locks (the locks that this method is reported not to work on) have serial numbers beginning with the number 800 on the back of the lock. Locks that do work are the locks with serial numbers beginning with 90, 01, 120 and five digit serial numbers, including those preceded by X's. However, I have heard it said that people are still opening these newer redesigned padlocks nonetheless. Also note: the same locks with keyholes in the back are also susceptible to this method. Those locks are made for schools so that school officials can inspect lockers. Either way, we are only picking locks for fun and or hobby, so if it doesn't work for you, it isn't like you are losing out on the market in reclaiming old padlocks with lost combinations. All those locks are collected at night by the lock gnomes and are never seen again.

Normal folks can contact Master Lock if they lost their number and Master Lock will give them their combination, but not without first providing the following excerpt from their website:

Due to increased security concerns nationwide, Master Lock recognizes the heightened need for additional safety measures. Effective immediately Master Lock will no longer provide lock combinations in response to phone, fax or e-mail requests. Master Lock realizes that these types of requests do not adequately prove ownership of the lock and puts you at additional risk. Please follow the procedure outlined below to obtain the combination to your lock:

- Print out the Lost Combination Form from a printer friendly page, or download the PDF file.
- Have your Lost Combination Form notarized by a Notary Public to prove that you are the owner of the lock.
- Photocopy the serial number on the back case of your combination lock.
- Mail the original completed, notarized Lost Combination Form and the photocopy of the back of your lock to the address below:

Master Lock Company
World Headquarters
137 W Forest Hill Ave.
PO Box 927
Oak Creek, WI 53154

(Considering the time and money that is involved in filling out the paperwork and then getting it notarized, you have to wonder just how much it's really worth it to replace a $5 lock. It makes me wonder if this isn't by design. You may see this and the rest of the web page at

http://www.masterlock.com/general/faqs_lostcom.shtml

In *Figure* 1.24, you will see a combination lock cut open to give you a quick view of the inside of this type of lock. You can see that there are three disks. The disk still in the lock case is attached to the handle or dial and it is the disk for the third number in the combination. We will discover the third number first and then we will discover the first number in the combination, and then the second in our hidden combination

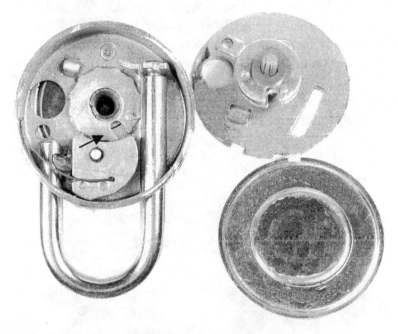

Figure 1.24 shows a combination padlock cut open

As you can see from *Figure* 1.24, there are three disks. The first that is attached to the dial has the groove cut out for the last number, (a black arrow is pointing to the groove) and the other two disks are grooved out for numbers one and two of the combination. For us to find the combination we will first need to find the last number in the combination and work backwards from there.

Let's begin:
With your Master combination lock in hand, turn the dial two turns to the right and stop at zero to clear the settings. Pull slightly up on the shackle (or down on the shackle if it is already locked around something), but not so tight that the dial can't move.

When trying to crack combination locks, a lot of attention is given to where the dial sticks. We will call those areas sticky spots. With Master Lock combinations, there are 12 sticky spots. As you can see from *Figure* 1.25 there are 11 fake sticky spots and one real one. The real sticky spot is the groove cut out of the disk. The lock mechanism will slide in the groove and allow the lock shackle to pull open.

Figure 1.25

Even though we are thinking in terms of opening the padlock based on numbers, it is the grooves that we are really concerned about.

Starting with the number 0 on the lock dial we are going to write the numbers associated with every sticky spot. There are 12 sticky spots so there will be twelve numbers. Now, let's pull on the shackle and turn the dial to the first sticky spot. On my padlock the first sticky spot moves between 0 and 1. This is a fake spot. The next spot wiggles between 3 and 4. This is another fake spot. The only numbers we care about writing down are the five sticky spots that wiggle between half way places, such as my next sticky spot at 6 ½ and 7 ½. Because the dial wiggles between both sides of 7, we want to keep this number, so we write it down. As you can see from the chart below, the next two sticky spots move from whole number to whole number and those are false. The next sticky spot moves between 16 ½ and 17 ½. This means the number is 17. Numbers 20 and 21 are fake and between 23 ½ and 24 ½ is the next sticky spot that wiggles between half spaces. We write down 24. As you can see our next two sticky spots on the halves are 27 and 37. As you can see by writing down all 5 sticky spots that dial between half numbers a definite pattern emerges. Four of the five numbers have a common number and one does not. It is this number that is dislike the others that is the correct number to the combination. We just found the last number in our 3 number combination. If you look at our next set of numbers in the diagram, you will see a similar pattern from another lock I used. The one number that stands out is also the last number in that padlock combination.

It is impossible for me to believe that this method of discovering the last number on the Master Lock combination lock is not by design. Perhaps the lock company, like many software programmers, simply left a backdoor on the lock.

After you study the diagram from *Figure* 1.24, and completely understand how we got the last number of the combination, we will move on to discover the next two numbers. If it helps, you can write down all 12 sticky spots.

Just remember, the sticky spots on the dial that wiggle between two line numbers are false. The sticky spots that wiggle between half lines, or the lines between the numbers are the digits that we are interested in.

Sticky Spots	Between Lines	Sticky Spots	Between Lines
0 – 1		3 – 4	
3 – 4		5 ½ – 6 ½	**6**
6 ½ – 7 ½	7	8 ½ – 9 ½	9
10 – 11		12 – 13	
13 – 14		15 – 16	
16 ½ – 17 ½	17	18 ½ – 19 ½	19
20 – 21		22 – 22	
23 ½ – 24 ½	**24**	25 – 26	
26 ½ – 27 ½	27	28 ½ – 29 ½	29
30 – 31		32 – 33	
33 – 34		35 – 36	
36 ½ – 37 ½	37	38 ½ – 39 ½	39

Figure 1.26 shows the results from two different combination padlocks using the sticky spot method. The darker numbers in the *Between Lines* columns are different from the other four numbers, and as a result is the number that we are looking for as the last number in our combination code. To discover the remaining numbers, we will use a modulus mathematical operator.

Discovering the missing numbers using modulus

Don't let the name 'modulus' scare you. The modulus operator is just dividing one number by another and the remainder is the modulus (it is also a severe condition that occurs when some computer people collect so many computer certifications they can no longer effectively work with computers and are forced to teach, but I can't back that up with any paper work, so please no e-mails.) This is going to be a little tricky, so you're going to need a piece of paper and something to write with.

Modulus Explained

Notation: (a % b) = c

This translates to: c as the remainder divided by b.

Examples: (33 % 4) = 1 or 4+4+4+4+4+4+4+4 = 32 with a remainder of 1. 1 is the modulus. Add the modulus to 32, which is how many 4's there are to 33 without going over and you will find 33.

(24 % 4) = 0 or six 4's with a 0 remainder. So our modulus is 0.

(7 % 4) = 3 There is one 4 in 7 without going over with a modulus or a remainder of 3. Together these two numbers equal our original.

The first number modulus 4 is the same as the last number modulus 4.

For example, let the last number of the lock be 24. Then (24 % 4) = 0, so we know that (first number % 4) = 0 as well. This means that the only possible values for the first number are: 0, 4, 8, 12, 16, 20, 24, 28, 32, and 36, because by adding 4 to 36 we arrive at 40, which is 0 on the dial.

(If you think that this is difficult to understand, try explaining it to someone)

Now with the modulus as 0, we count by 4 with only 10 possible numbers for the first number on our combination lock. So I know that my last number is 24 and my first number is one of 0, 4, 8, 12, 16, 20, 24, 28, 32, and 36, because I divided 24 into 4 and had 0 as a remainder.

Lets write down the numbers that you derived from the modulus on your lock and put them away for right now.

Note: There are only ten possibilities. This is because the dial only has 40 marks, and by enforcing the modulus operator we essentially are dividing the possibilities by 4. Try this out on your own lock, and verify that the (first number % 4) equals the (last number % 4).

The Second Number of the Combination

The second number modulus 4 is the last number modulus 4 plus or minus 2.

If the last number modulus 4 is 0, then the second number modulus 4 is 2, and vice versa. If the last number modulus 4 is 1, than the second number modulus 4 is 3, and vice versa. Why? Because we are going to add the number 2 to the modulus in our first number.

(If the reason for this is confusing, just don't worry about understanding it right now and just add 2 to the modulus from our first number that we found for our combination. It's not important that you understand it at the moment; just follow the steps and it will become clearer later).

Let's continue our example from above with the last number equal to 24. (24 % 4) = 0, so the second number modulus 4 is equal to 2. This means that the possible values for the second number are 2, 6, 10, 14, 18, 22, 26, 30, 34, and 38. Again note that there are only ten possibilities. Try this out on your own lock, and verify that the (second number % 4) = (last number % 4) plus or minus 2.

First Number: 0, 4, 8, 12, 16, 20, 24, 28, 32, or 36.

Second Number: 2, 6, 10, 14, 18, 22, 26, 30, 34, or 38

Last Number: 24

Now it's Time to do Some Work...

You're thinking about padlock shims right now, aren't you? Stop it! Still got that piece of paper? Good. You're going to need it. For those of you who made it this far, our next step is to try every possible combination from our list of numbers above. Below I took the liberty of printing out all possible combinations from the numbers that we extrapolated. There are only 100 possible combinations and it doesn't take a long as you might think. Yes, that's right; you have to try every possible combination using our numbers. You might even get lucky and find the correct number in the first 10 combinations.

- *Remember* to turn the dial RIGHT, LEFT two times around and then RIGHT directly to the last number.

0 - 2 - 24	12 - 14 - 24	24 - 26 - 24
0 - 6 - 24	12 - 18 - 24	24 - 30 - 24
0 - 10 - 24	12 - 22 - 24	24 - 34 - 24
0 - 14 - 24	12 - 26 - 24	24 - 38 - 24
0 - 18 - 24	12 - 30 - 24	28 - 2 - 24
0 - 22 - 24	12 - 34 - 24	28 - 6 - 24
0 - 26 - 24	12 - 38 - 24	28 - 10 - 24
0 - 30 - 24	16 - 2 - 24	28 - 14 - 24

0 - 34 - 24	16 - 6 - 24	28 - 18 - 24
0 - 38 - 24	16 - 10 - 24	28 - 22 - 24
4 - 2 - 24	16 - 14 - 24	28 - 26 - 24
4 - 6 - 24	16 - 18 - 24	28 - 30 - 24
4 - 10 - 24	16 - 22 - 24	28 - 34 - 24
4 - 14 - 24	16 - 26 - 24	28 - 38 - 24
4 - 18 - 24	16 - 30 - 24	32 - 2 - 24
4 - 22 - 24	16 - 34 - 24	32 - 6 - 24
4 - 26 - 24	16 - 38 - 24	32 - 10 - 24
4 - 30 - 24	20 - 2 - 24	32 - 14 - 24
4 - 34 - 24	20 - 6 - 24	32 - 18 - 24
4 - 38 - 24	20 - 10 - 24	32 - 22 - 24
8 - 2 - 24	20 - 14 - 24	32 - 26 - 24
8 - 6 - 24	20 - 18 - 24	32 - 30 - 24
8 - 10 - 24	20 - 22 - 24	32 - 34 - 24
8 - 14 - 24	20 - 26 - 24	32 - 38 - 24
8 - 18 - 24	20 - 30 - 24	36 - 2 - 24
8 - 22 - 24	20 - 34 - 24	36 - 6 - 24
8 - 26 - 24	20 - 38 - 24	36 - 10 - 24
8 - 30 - 24	24 - 2 - 24	36 - 14 - 24
8 - 34 - 24	24 - 6 - 24	36 - 18 - 24
8 - 38 - 24	24 - 10 - 24	36 - 22 - 24
12 - 2 - 24	24 - 14 - 24	36 - 26 - 24
12 - 6 - 24	24 - 18 - 24	36 - 30 - 24
12 - 10 - 24	24 - 22 - 24	36 - 34 - 24
		36 - 38 - 24

There are 100 possible combinations that can take anywhere from two minutes to 30 minutes depending on your eye hand coordination. This combination took me 80 tries and 15 minutes to crack the code. (28-38–24) With this combination lock I found the right numbers on my 80th try. I've done others in under ten and less than three minutes. There is no doubt that there is some time involved in finding the combination using this method, and a padlock shim will work much, much faster. And because you have read down this far, I will give you instructions on how to open a combination lock with shims. But first I want to thank Rob Nason, who posted the math behind this on Harvard's website. After thinking of all the ways I've tried to understand this, his was the easiest to understand. So, thanks Rob.

Opening a Combination Lock with a Padlock Shim

Now, opening a combination lock with a padlock shim. You will need the largest shim you have to open a combination lock padlock, because of how deep the latch that holds down the shackle. You will need to slide the shim on the outside on the right hand side of the shackle. Slowly turn the shim until it is on the inside. You must wedge the shim between the shackle and the latch, as shown in *Figure* 1.26. The white arrow indicates that the shim has been successfully seated and the shackle can be pulled and unlocked. If the shim rises up during the turn, as in many cases it does, you will have to begin again. It is a delicate procedure sliding the padlock shim in and exerting enough force without bending it. You have to simply twist, wiggle and push the shim down and to the side until you can pull the shake out. The fastest that I've ever opened a combination lock with a shim has been 10 seconds. On the same lock a few days later it took me 4 minutes to open. Some days you surprise yourself with just how fast you are, while others you don't know what you're doing wrong.

"Some days you're the statue, while others you are the pigeon." *--Men's room wall*

Figure 1.26 shows a padlock shim wedged between the shackle and blocking the latch from engaging.

If you are not able to use the shims right away, don't be discouraged. Like everything, it takes practice and patience. I've given away a pair of padlock shims to a friend and the next time I saw him he told me that he tried to impress some people by opening a padlock, but the shims didn't work. I asked if you slid down both ends shackles? And he replied, "both?" Whether he did or not isn't really the point. The fact of the matter is he tried to use them without ever practicing.

I also must warn you that padlock shims are a little tough on the hands at first, just like picking a lock. Until your fingers can build up the strength, in the beginning you are going to be a little sore. And after all, like I've said before, this is just for fun and sport. Unless you are going to seriously make a career out of being a locksmith, or until lock picking becomes an Olympic event, I wouldn't be too harsh on yourself if you don't immediately get it your first few tries.

Picking Deadbolts

Figure 1.27 shows two deadbolts

It's a little disconcerting when you discover just how easy it is to pick a deadbolt lock open (I mean to say, with practice). Some lock pickers claim that a deadbolt is easier than picking a padlock, even less difficulty than it takes a high school kid to exploit a Windows operating system vulnerability in a computer lab, and just slightly harder than inserting a file from a pair of finger nail clippers into a desk drawer and jiggling them around like a crazy person. Picking a deadbolt is not only easy, it is frighteningly easy because this is the lock that protects all of your valuables and your family.

Note: I restate that I'm only referring to cheap deadbolts. There are many high security deadlocks that are near impossible to pick. However, 80 percent of deadbolts used in residential doors are the cheap deadbolts.

Writing this chapter bothered me so much that I added extra locks and latches to every opening in my house. As I'm sure you will consider as well.

Deadbolts share the same similarities as padlocks do with the exception that sometimes they have more pins. Deadbolts might have five pins or more, depending on the style and price.

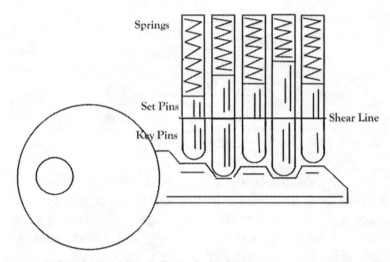

Figure 1.28 shows a basic five pin lock set up.

The two most popular deadbolts that you will find in your house are either a Kwickset or Schlage. The popularity of these locks is attributed to their prices, and contractors use them because they are very affordable. The more affordable a lock the easier it is to pick. Kwickset is the most affordable deadbolt in my area, and I dare to say the entire United States. There are more expensive and secure deadbolts, but as this book is meant as a beginner's guide to learning the sport of lock picking, let's first learn how to pick the easy locks before we move up to a more advanced level of lock picking.

Upon one of my many trips to the hardware store, I purchased both the Kwickset and the Schlage deadbolt. That evening I sat down in front of the television and picked the Kwickset immediately. I'd say in less than one minute. Surprised and a little disappointed that the lock opened so quickly, I tried again. The second time took only a few seconds more. I should say that it's not uncommon to pick a lock right off the bat, and not be able to do it again or take a considerable longer amount of time. On my second try I did it in less than two minutes again. The challenge from that lock was lost almost immediately and forever. So I tossed it into my box of locks and moved on to the next.

Note:

I have heard that some people will upon successfully picking a lock, return it in exchange for another. I'm not suggesting that you do that, but that is what some people do...that is all. Personally, I like to keep them as trophies. However, I make a good enough living and can afford to waste money on foolish nonsense that collects dust in a box (you can tell that my wife helped edit this book).

The Schlage deadbolt took a little more time to open on the first attempt, but it still opened in under ten minutes. Ten minutes of lock picking actually feels a lot longer. I immediately moved to the deadbolts on my doors and then gave serious contemplation to getting large dogs for the house. Someone might be less likely to pick your house locks if on the other side of the door was Mad Max with foaming mouth fever waiting to kill.

Deadbolts installed upside down are the hardest to pick, as you will discover when you are able to hold one in your hands, fresh out of the box. Some countries install locks upside down as a standard. An upside down lock prevents the bottom pins from falling freely and out of the way when the top pins are set. Locksmiths will say that the most difficult locks to pick are the ones where people have locked their children inside their car with the engine on. The parents are usually frantic, and if you don't get it within the first few seconds they help speed the process along by yelling at you.

Figure 1.29 compares the plug of a padlock to a deadbolt

Hint:
Which Direction Do I Turn The Plug?

To unlock most deadbolts, if the bolt is protruding to the left then the plug must rotate clockwise. If the bolt is protruding to the right, then the plug must rotate counter-clockwise. The opposite is therefore true to lock the deadbolt. Another way to tell is simply by turning the plug to see which direction turns the most.

Torque?

The right amount of tension with your torque wrench is the "key" to lock picking, but when you are new to this hobby, it's difficult to know the right amount of tension. The wrong tension is often the number one reason for lock picking failure. If you apply too much tension to the plug, the pins will be bound too tight and you will not be about to push them through into their respective chambers. If you don't feel any pin action then you are probably exerting too much force on the torque wrench. Simply release the tension and re-insert your pick. Apply just enough tension to feel the pins bind slightly, maintain tension and continue pushing pins.

Best Pick Methods and Troublesome Locks

Personally speaking, the best pick method is the method that works best for you. I like to start off raking the pins with a rake pick, then I will switch to my half-diamond head pick and try pressing in the remaining pins. If that doesn't work I will then begin rocking, or bouncing my pick back and forth. If the lock isn't open by then, I use a large hook pick and fiddle around with the first pin at the opening of the key way. That usually does the trick.

There are times when I have deployed all three methods, reverted back to the rake, reached for the pick guns and still nothing has happened. Impatience will often cause me to release all tension and begin again. Once the tension is released, you can hear all the pins spring back out again. You ask yourself, was that five pins or six? You immediately begin again and are stuck in the same situation. What usually gets me past this point is when I use a dental instrument given to me by a friend who is a dentist, (you know, the gum hook pointy thing) and press every pin.

This usually does the trick. With many troublesome locks, the problem is usually a high pin blocking your ability to press a smaller pin directly onto the other side of it. It's not likely that you will get one of these same dental instruments, but you can improvise. And with lock picking, improvisation is 90 percent of the fun. Paper clips are the locksmith's friend. A simple paper clip can be bent into most shapes and will still maintain a solid poke. In the next Figure you will find a repeat of pin types to help give you a mental picture of what pins really look like.

Picking a Deadbolt

Picking a deadbolt is in many ways the same as picking a padlock. There is a shear line, (or two if it is a commercial deadbolt with a master key) bottom pins, top pins, top pin springs and a plug. When the key enters the key way, it presses the pins to the exact level needed to set them evenly with the shear line and still allow the key to turn, as shown in *Figure* 1.30.

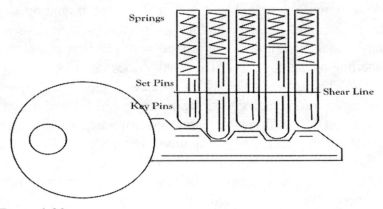

Figure 1.30

Here is a repeat of several security pins for a visual aid.

The pins shown below are high security pins that have been fabricated to prevent picking. From the top left and across, these pins are. 1. *Medeco bottom pin*, 2. *Schlage bottom pin*, 3. *Medeco mushroom pin*, 4. *Serrated pin*, 5. *American pin*, 6. *Spool pin*.

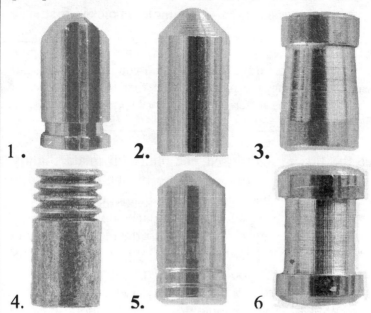

As you can see each pin is designed to show how conventional pin binding is used to pick a lock. There is one tool that is used to over come this issue, and that is a feather spring torque wrench, shown below. This spring device gently binds the pin while you push them into place. You will still need to use a turning tool to turn the plug. The spring wrench is only for setting it.

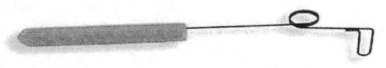

One of the best ways to determine the greatest resistance to the pins is by touch. Insert your torque wrench, or whatever turning tool you are using, into the key way of a lock. Apply and maintain turning pressure on the plug, while using your picking tool to gently move each of the pins one at a time. The tumbler that has the most difficulty moving has the greatest resistance. This tumbler is picked first.

Note: It really makes no difference in which direction you pick, whether it's from the front or back. When you first apply turning pressure to the plug, the pins that grab first will dictate where you begin. It can be different with every lock, even in the same model due to manufacturing flaws.

Once the first pin is picked, the plug will rotate slightly. While maintaining turning pressure on the plug, the next pin or two, will become wedged inside the shear line. Something to also remember is, as each top pin is pushed into place as the plug turns, you must decide if the bounce of the bottom pin (or bottom pin) is by gravity or from the top pin spring. If you look back at *Figure* 1.30, you will see that the key and top pin are forced down the hull by a spring. With time you can feel whether the bottom pin is falling because of gravity, or the pressure from the opposing spring above it.

With the first pin set, you may or may not have felt the plug move. Sometimes in the beginning it is difficult to tell. Sometimes we will put too much force on the torque wrench, and the pins will not move. If you begin to notice that your pick is bending at the end or beginning to warp, you are probably applying too much force to your turning tool. Just ease up a bit. I broke my first picks in the first week due to using too much force. So you will have to practice with different levels of pressure until you get it right.

Now we begin setting the next pin in place. We push up on the pins like we did the first one until the plug turns ever so slightly again. Then the next pin and the next until all pins are set and we open the lock. Sounds too easy? It is. I will take a guess and say that in the beginning, half of you will get it right away, while the others will have to be more persistent.

The first deadbolt that I picked was the one on my laundry room door. I was determined, but very unsuccessful. Every night for four days in a row I failed to pick the lock. Only after purchasing a couple of cheap deadbolts from the hardware store, and practicing with them, was I able to return to the garage door and pick that lock. To my surprise, the garage door lock was the exact lock I bought and picked on my first try. So, I wasn't one of those people that got it right away.

Different Picking Methods:

I'm going to repeat different methods of picking to help those of you that are having trouble. There are three types of picking methods generally used to pick a lock: Pin pressing, Bouncing, and Scrubbing (some people also refer to this as Raking). Sometimes I employ all three methods.

- Pin pressing is when you use a diamond headed pick and gently push the pins up past the shear line and into the hull.
- Scrubbing, or Raking, is when you use a rake pick and run it really fast back and forth against the pins. You might rotate between raking back and forth to a scrubbing circular motion.

- Bouncing is when you insert your pick into the key way and gently rock the tip of your tool up and down and you move back and forth against the pins, while applying minimal tension using your torque wrench.

Remember that the purpose of your torque wrench is to bind a pin in the shear line so you can push into its slot. If you pull back and do not maintain constant pressure, the pins that you've successfully pushed into place will fall back down past the shear line and you will have to start over again. When executed correctly with the right amount of torque and correctly pushing in your pins you will be successful. If you have the key to the lock, examine it, count the grooves on the key and look how far they go back into the keyway.

If you don't get it right away, just be patient and keep practicing until you do get it. Once you gain the confidence of opening your first lock, the rest just seems to come easier.

Picking Wafer Locks

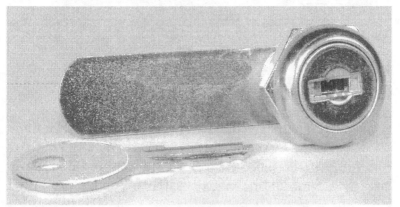

Figure 1.31 shows a standard cabinet / drawer wafer lock

There are several different types of wafer locks. They range from a basic cabinet lock to a car ignition. The simplest to pick is of course the cabinet, desk drawer and utility lock variety. Because we are not going to get into auto lock picking, I will keep all my references to the type of locks found on cabinets and desk

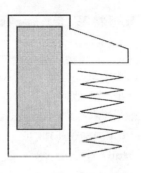

drawers. Wafer locks are different than pins and tumbler locks because they use small wafer-shaped pins in place of tumbler pins, as shown in the figure above. (But a wafer lock is still pickable in the same manner as a pin tumbler lock.) The rake pick is the tool most often used to pick a single-sided wafer lock. Like the pins in a pin tumbler, wafers slide up and down. Another main difference is that there are no top pins in a wafer lock. There are only flat wafers driven by a small spring. It is the inside of the wafers that makes the height of the pins. The wafers are cut out at different levels as shown in *Figure* 1.32.

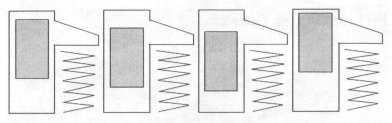

Figure 1.32 shows how wafers are cut for key heights.

When a key is inserted that matches the heights of the wafer cut outs, the shear line is cleared and the plug can turn to open the lock. If this were a double-sided wafer lock, the key would be cut for wafers on both sides of the key. .

Double Wafer Locks

Double wafer locks are locks with the wafers on the top and bottom and require a double-sided key. You may use your tumbler pin lock picks, but double-sided lock picks are available for fewer than ten dollars on the Internet. In addition to double-sided picks, there are also double-sided torque wrenches.

Figure 1.33 shows a double-sided pick.

The reason I haven't gone into too much detail about how to use these tools or how to pick a wafer lock is because most people just use the file on a pair of fingernail clippers. However, if you must know…

With single-sided picking tools on a single-sided wafer:

Insert your torque wrench, and then insert your single-sided picks, wiggle frantically while turning your torque wrench and open.

With single-sided picking tools on a double-sided wafer:

Insert your torque wrench, and then insert your single-sided picks, wiggle frantically while turning your torque wrench and open.

With double-sided picking tools on a double-sided wafer:

Insert your double-side torque wrench, and then insert your double-sided picks, wiggle frantically while turning your torque wrench and open.

Using the file from a pair of fingernail clippers:

Open your pair of fingernail clippers, retract the small nail file, insert the file into the single or double-sided wafer lock, and wiggle frantically while turning and it will open.

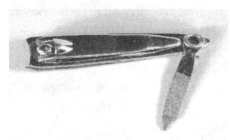

Figure 1.34 shows an average pair of fingernail clippers.

Magnetic Locks

Magnetic locks are as their name suggests locks that use magnets. A magnetic key is set with several small magnetic fields that, when lined up with the lock/unlock mechanism, will repel the other magnets inside the lock causing the spring-loaded bolt to open the lock. See *Figure* 1.35.

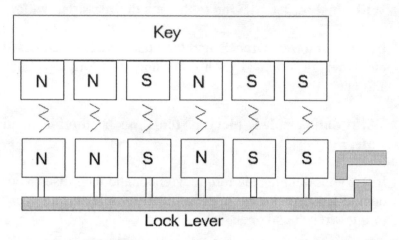

Figure 1.35 shows the poles of a magnetic key (that repel each other) lining up with the lock lever.

As you can see from *Figure* 1.35, when the same magnetic poles come in contact with each other, by nature they push away, or repel. As the key enters the guided key way and lines up with its magnetic counterpart, the lock lever moves back and away from the key and the latch that locks into place. There are magnetic picks with a combination of North and South pole fields that you run in and out of the key way, while using a torque wrench, in hopes of repelling all the magnets away to free the latch. There is also a method of using a pulsating electromagnetic field that will cause the magnets in the lock to vibrate above 20 vibrations per second. This allows for a sporadic jerking motion on the bolt that will allow the handle to turn. This method of using a pulsating electromagnetic device can also cause the small magnets to change their magnetic pole direction. In other words, your lock would have to be reset or replaced by a locksmith.

Tubular Lock Picking

Tubular locks are the types of locks you see on vending machines. The key way is round and the plug is in the center, as shown in *Figure* 1.36.

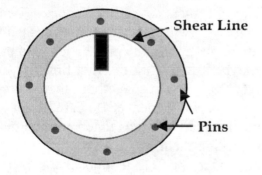

Figure 1.36 shows an illustration of a tubular style lock. The center circle is the plug and the outer circle is where the pins and shear line resides.

Tubular locks use the pin-tumbler and wafer-tumbler method of lock design, but instead of on rows of pins, the pins on a tubular lock have pins positioned all the way around the circumference of the cylinder-shaped plug. It takes a special type of pick to pick a tubular lock. There are several types of tubular lock picks. *Figure* 1.37 shows one such type of tubular pick.

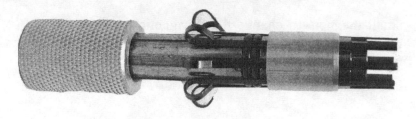

Figure 1.37 shows an 8-finger tubular lock pick.

To use the lock pick, you must first pull all of the pick fingers back towards the handle. The pick fingers are the black hairpin-looking objects in *Figure* 1.37. Once this is done, insert the round pick end into the circle lock. Slide one pick finger at a time into the lock until all picks are inserted. Try to keep the pick as perpendicular as you possibly can, otherwise you will have to start over again. Once all the picks are in place, turn the pick handle and the lock should open. Maybe it will work the first time maybe it won't. Like every lock picking method that we've discussed, it takes practice and patience. Be careful not to remove the brass ring that holds the pins together like I did, otherwise you'll be picking them up all over the floor (if you can find them all) and trying to fit them back together.

I've read where some people who are into making their own tools will fabricate a tubular lock pick from bits of pipe, picks and rubber bands. I'm not suggesting that you do this, in fact, I'm not even suggesting that you should even want to pick a tubular lock. But if you do, you'll need bits of pipe, some hairpins and I suppose a good sturdy rubber band.

Anyway...

Push Button Combination Locks

Push button combination locks, or puzzle locks as some computer people like to call them, are the locks that you might see on your server room door, or even some of the office doors where you work. Because of the wide variety of these locks, I'm only going to address the five button locks, as they seem to be the most widely used. And really the only reason I mention it is because most computer people have to confront these types of locks on a daily basis.

There is a lot of material on the Internet about how to open five button combination locks, most of what you will find doesn't work. If for some preposterous reason you can't get into your server room door because someone has changed the combination, minutes after being fired you have only three real choices. Drill out the lock, climb over the ceiling tiles, or guess the combination. If none of these are an option, then your only other option is cracking the code. How do you crack the code on a five-button combination? Well, I hope you're in a comfortable position because this is going to take a while...

There are several brands of push button combination locks out there, but the ones that I am familiar with are the Simplex or Unican locks. Before we begin, a friend of mine, Chucklz, from lockpicking101.com suggested that before I walk you through this, that you try to use the factory set combination [24] 3. "Locks are like computers... many times the user is too lazy to change the default password (groan)."

The thing about most push button locks is that you can set the combination by pressing one number at a time or three. In other words, you can push more than one button at a time. So your combination can be: 1 | 2 | 3 | 4 or

1 | 2 3 | 4. In *Figure* 1.38 you will see a combination of four buttons that need to be pressed to complete the code.

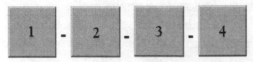

Figure 1.38 shows a combination that requires four buttons to be pressed in a row.

In *Figure* 1.39, you see a combination with only three presses because 2 and 3 must be pressed at the same time.

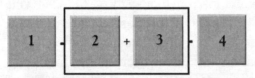

Figure 1.39 shows a three push combination, where the 2 and 3 need to be pressed at the same time.

So the code on a five-button combination press button lock can be set by using 1 thru 5 or all of the numbers, or by pressing a combination of a single number mixed with pressing two or three numbers at the same time. You could set your code to be 1 |3 4 2 | 5, if you'd like. There are certainly a lot of different combinations of numbers to choose from, 1,081 to be exact. And like passwords, I bet there are only a handful of codes selected. As people seem to follow the same suit with picking a code. Of course there is no way to ever prove it.

There is a method of discovering the unknown numbers of a five-button combination lock by pressing each number while the knob is fully turned. The button that gives the least resistance is said to be a number in the code. If the lock has a lever, the correct buttons are said to wiggle the latch. On some locks this may work, but for the most part these methods are not reliable enough to give too much detail to in this book.

1,081 different combinations

Let's just assume for a moment that there was no magic way to crack a push button combination lock and you were forced to go through all 1,081 combinations. Certainly I'm not suggesting that there isn't a way to crack the code, I'm just saying, if there is, I wish I knew what it was because I don't and now we have to go through all 1,081 combinations until we find the missing number on our server room door.

Note: There are a lot of reported ways to crack the code on a 5-button Simplex push button combination lock, but I haven't found any of them to be particularly successful or truthful.

I have heard that if one were to sit down and punch in every possible combination on a five-button combination lock that it will take somewhere close to four hours. And this is only if the unknown number was the very last. If your number is within the first 540 punches, then you are only looking at two hours. If you are the unlucky type whose number is always closer to the end, then it is possible that if you started backwards from the list of possible numbers you could conceivably find the right combination immediately. But then again, because you are so unlucky that you started in reverse, the number would more likely be in the beginning of the list and you're right back at four hours. If this sounds like you, you might consider having one of your lucky friends do this instead.

Like I said earlier, there are 1,081 possible combinations to opening a five-button combination lock. If you have the patience or are simply too "big" to climb over the ceiling tiles, then go to *Appendix D* at the back of this book and you will find a list of every possible combination for a five-button combination lock.

Appendix A

Tools & Miscellaneous Items

A Pick Gun

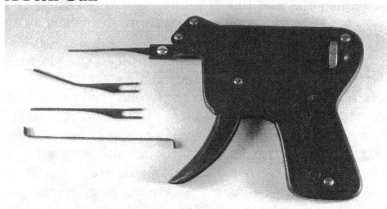

Figure 1.34 shows a pick gun with 3 standard picks and a torque wrench.

Using a pick gun is a technique in itself. As you can see from *Figure* 1.34, there are different pick angles and you still need to use a torque wrench to bind the pins. If you look at the top right of the pick gun, you will see an adjustment screw. This screw is used to adjust the amount of pressure in the snap of the gun. Before we talk about how to use the gun, let's first talk about what the gun does.

As we have already learned, the top pins have to clear the shear line in order for the plug to turn. With hand picks we set the pins manually by pressing them, or scrubbing them into place while using a turning tool to apply force on the pins that are caught in the 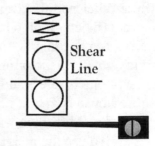 shear line. The only thing that changes in this technique is the picks. We have exchanged a hand pick for a spring loaded picking gun. The idea behind using the pick gun can be explained by what happens when two pool balls are placed beside each other when they touch. When the cue ball strikes one ball, the energy of the impact is transferred through the first ball and causes the second ball to go flying across the pool table. If you imagine that the pins in a lock are like pool balls and when the pick on the pick gun snaps quickly and violently upwards, the energy from the strike passes through the first pin and sends the second pin into it's hull.

Warning about tension strengths on the pick gun:

Always start with the weakest setting when using these guns and work your way up from there. Some cheaper locks tend to have weaker springs. If your pick strikes with too much force, it makes it more difficult to pick the lock.

As you can see in *Figure* 1.34, there are two different angles of picks. The first pick is straight and the other is at an angle. From my own experience I have found that the straight pick, held level in the key way works better for picking the lock than using it on an angle. I know some people prefer to use the angle pick.

I personally don't like to use the pick gun at all, while other people swear by it. They say that it is a faster more efficient tool when you have to open a lock in a hurry. Maybe this is true if you are a locksmith and are trying to get a door open because your customer locked herself out in the middle of cooking dinner and now the entire house is at risk of burning down, but as a hobbyist, I prefer the old fashion way.

To use the pick gun you simply insert the pick at the top of the key way and slide it in all the way until it stops at the back plate of the door lock. Now insert your torque wrench into the base of the key way, and beginning with the weakest setting on the gun, begin clicking your butt off.

Click, Click, Click, Click, Click, Click…

Remember to hold your gun as level as you can so the length of the pick is striking the pins and not the tip. Your objective is the same as with the hand picks; you are trying to set the top pins above the shear line, so you will need to continue to maintain pressure with your turning tool.

If at first you are not successful, don't be easily discouraged. This method of lock picking, like all methods, just takes time, patience, and practice. Nothing anyone picks up quickly stays with him or her, as they usually become bored and move on to something more challenging. If the plug hasn't turned after ten clicks, try repositioning the gun by sliding it out towards you and then back in again. If after 30 clicks and you're still not successful, and live with someone, it's not likely that you'll make it past 50 clicks as your spouse or roommate will most assuredly take the pick gun away from you and storm back off into the other room from which they came.

Cordless Vibrating Lock Picks

Cordless Vibrating Lock Picks are just that. They are cordless, they vibrate and you can use them to pick a lock. What more were you expecting me to say? Like the pick gun, the vibration of the pick causes the top pin to jump, or dance above the bottom pin. Remember you still need to use a turning tool because the basic principles of picking a pin tumbler lock still apply. The cordless vibrating lock picks are faster, more expensive and for certain individuals, can help make a lonely night a little less lonely.

There I said it. You know you were thinking it anyways.

Jigglers

A thin piece of metal cut in the general shape of a key. Like the names suggests, a jiggler is inserted into the key way and is jiggled around in hopes of opening the lock. Jigglers come in a variety of general cuts that vaguely resemble cuts on keys.

Lock Scopes

A lock scope is a lot like one of those instruments a doctor puts in your ear and looks to see if you have an infection. A locksmith will use a scope to look into a lock and examine the key way for obstruction, or to visibly count how many pins are inside.

Spinners

A plug spinner is used when you pick a lock in the wrong direction and need to move the plug to the other side of the shear line without picking it again.

Codebook

A codebook is the little black book with all the codes that link the numbers on keys to the correct corresponding pin. In other words, a locksmith would take the number from the lock and use it to cut a key to fit the lock. Listed below are different sources for codebooks:

HPC: Windows based codebook for under $700.

Locksmith Ledger: DOS version only, $699.95. No copy protection.

Blackhawk Products: DOS and Windows version for under $500

Genericode: Reeds Codes on a disk

Treskat: DOS based program also under $500

Appendix B

Terms and References
Special Thanks to Varjeal from Lockpicking101.com

Backplate: The plate on the inside of a door through which the cylinder connecting screws and tailpiece is passed.

Backset: The horizontal distance from the edge of a door to the center of the lockset.

Bi-lock: A pin tumbler cylinder lock consisting of two parallel rows of pin tumblers and two sidebars operated by a U-shaped key.

Bit key: A key with a bit projecting from a solid cylindrical shaft. The bit has cuts to bypass the wards or operate levers in the correct lock.

Bit key lock: A warded or lever lock that uses bit keys.

Bitting: A cut, or series of cuts, on the bit or blade of a key.

Blade: The portion of the key that is inserted into the lock.

Blank: A key before any cuts have been made.

Bottom Pins: The pins that the key touches

Bow: The handle of the key.

Bypass tool: Any device that bypasses the manufacturer's designed method for opening the lock. A pick or shim is considered a bypass tool.

Cam lock: A lock that has an attached cam that serves as the lock's bolt. Cam locks are often used on cabinets, file cabinets and drawers. *See Wafer lock*.

Case: The housing or body of a lock.

Case ward: Protrusions on the sides of the key way to allow entry of only the correct type of key blank.

Change index: The point on a key changeable combination lock dial ring to which the old and new combinations must be dialed when changing the combination.

Change key: The key that operates one lock in a master keyed system.

Cylindrical Lock - A lock whose tumblers are positioned perpendicular to the key way.

Control key: A key used to remove the core of an interchangeable core cylinder.

Control sleeve: The part of an interchangeable core-retaining device that surrounds the plug.

Cross-bore: A hole drilled into the face of a door where a bored or interconnected lockset is to be installed.

Cuts: A cut, or series of cuts, on the bit or blade of a key.

Cylinder key: A key for use with pin tumbler and wafer tumbler cylinder locks.

Deadbolt: A lock bolt that is turned into the doorjamb where it is locked in to place. A deadbolt typically doesn't have any spring action and is manually driven.

Deadlock: A lock that projects a deadbolt.

Double-acting lever tumbler: A tumbler that must be lifted to a precise level, not too little or too much to allow movement of a bolt.

Double cylinder: Pertaining to a lock with two keyed cylinders.

Double cylinder deadlock: A deadbolt lock whose bolt may be operated by a key from either side.

Grooves: Long narrow ridges milled out areas along the sides of the key blade to allow the blade to bypass the wards in the keyway.

Heel & toe locking: Describes a padlock that has locking dogs at both the heel and toe of the shackle. The notches cut into the base of the shackle.

Heel (of a padlock shackle): The part of a padlock shackle that is kept in the case when in the unlocked position.

Hook bolt: A lock bolt that is shaped like a hook. This is normally used on sliding doors.

Impressioning: is what locksmiths do with a blank in a keyway. Marks left on the blank determine the necessary cut of the key.

Interconnected lockset: A lockset whose trim provides a means of simultaneous retraction of two or more bolts that may also be operated independently.

Jamb: The inside vertical face of a doorway.

Jiggler: A thin piece of metal cut in the general shape of a key. A jiggler will slip into the key way of most locks. Like the name suggests, you jiggle a jiggler in the key way in hopes of opening the lock.

Key code: A series of numbers or digits on a key or lock that specifies or references the particular cuts of the key to operate a lock.

Keyway: The part of the plug where you insert the key.

Keyway grooves: Long narrow milled out areas along the sides of the blade to allow the blade to bypass the wards in the keyway.

Latch: A mechanical device, which automatically keeps a door closed until a deliberate action is used to retract it.

Lever lock: Lock with levers that are each lifted to the correct level by a bit key or flat metal key to enable the lock to operate.

Lock: Any device that secures the access or entry to personal property.

Locksmith: A person with the knowledge and profession to install, service and bypass locks.

Lower pins: The pins of a lock that contact the cuts on the key. Also called Key Pins.

Mushroom pin - A specialty top pin that has a shape closely resembling a mushroom. This type of pin binds in the shear line and gives a false feeling of accomplishment.

Picking tool – Any tool that can be used to manipulate the tumblers of a lock and open it.

Plug: The part of the lock that you put the key into and turn to operate the lock.

Pin stack: The combination of a lower pin sitting beneath an upper pin. A lock that has a master key has a set of additional master pins and allows for two shear lines.

Rim lock: A lock or latch typically mounted on the surface of a door or drawer.

Shackle: The U-shaped part of a padlock.

Shear line: The dividing line between the plug and the shell that when free of pins is allowed to turn.

Shell: The outer part of the lock that surrounds the plug.

Shoulder: The edge of the key that touches the face of the lock to define how far the key is inserted into the lock.

Single-acting lever tumbler: A lever tumbler which must be moved a minimum distance to allow travel of a bolt, but cannot be moved so far as to restrict travel of the bolt.

Skeleton key: Any non-cylinder key that is used to open locks with mechanical levers.

Spool Pin - A specialty pin whose shape resembles a spool of thread. This type of pin adds pick resistance to the lock.

Tip: The very end of the key that you stick into the lock first.

Toe (of a shackle): That part of the shackle that may be removed from the padlock body.

Top Pins: The pins in a lock that sits on top of the lower pins and rest against the springs. Also known as Set Pins.

Tubular key cylinder: A cylinder whose tumblers are arranged in a circle and which is operated by a tubular key.

Tubular lockset: A bored lockset whose latch or bolt locking mechanism is contained in the component installed into the edge bore.

Tumbler - A moveable obstruction of varying size and configuration in a lock that makes direct contact with the key or another tumbler and prevents an incorrect key or torque device from activating the lock or other mechanism. Commonly known as pins or wafers (disks).

Wafer - Disks of varying shapes and sizes positioned within the shell and plug of a cylindrical lock.

Ward: (as in warded locks) Protrusions that stick out of the sides of the keyway to restrict entry to the correct type of key blank.

Appendix C

Links On The Internet

The Network Administrator.com
http://www.thenetworkadministrator.com

Extreme Media
"Your source for information on hard to find subjects"
HackersCatalog.com

LPCon FAQ:
http://www.worldwidewardrive.org/dclp/LPCONFAQ.html

LPCon Rules and Registration:
http://www.worldwidewardrive.org/dclp/DCLP.html

DefCon
http://www.defcon.org/

Lock Picking 101
http://www.lockpicking101.com

The Open Organisation of Lockpickers
www.toool.nl
http://connect.waag.org/toool/

dc719.org
http://www.dc719.org/

SpyHeadQuarters
www.spyhq.com

Sportenthusiasts of Lockpicking – Europe
www.lockpicking.org

Lock Picks.com
http://www.lockpicks.com/store.asp

Lock Pick Tools.net
http://lockpicktools.net/

Pick Sets.com
http://pick-sets.com

The Great Philadelphia Locksmith Association
http://www.gpla.org/

The New York Association of In-house Locksmiths, Inc.
http://www.locksmith.org/

HPC World Locksmith Tool Maker
http://www.hpcworld.com/

Westthorn House Software
http://www.whsoftware.com/

Appendix D

The 1,081 possible combinations of a five-button combination lock.

1						2&5	4			
1	2					2&5	4	1		
1	2	3				2&5	4	1	3	
1	2	3	4			2&5	4	1&3		
1	2	3	4	5		2&5	4	3		
1	2	3	4&5			2&5	4	3	1	
1	2	3	5			3				
1	2	3	5	4		3	1			
1	2	3&4				3	1	2		
1	2	3&4	5			3	1	2	4	
1	2	3&4&5				3	1	2	4	5
1	2	3&5				3	1	2	4&5	
1	2	3&5	4			3	1	2	5	
1	2	4				3	1	2	5	4
1	2	4	3			3	1	2&4		
1	2	4	3	5		3	1	2&4	5	
1	2	4	3&5			3	1	2&4&5		
1	2	4	5			3	1	2&5		
1	2	4	5	3		3	1	2&5	4	
1	2	4&5				3	1	4		
1	2	4&5	3			3	1	4	2	
1	2	5				3	1	4	2	5
1	2	5	3			3	1	4	2&5	
1	2	5	3	4		3	1	4	5	
1	2	5	3&4			3	1	4	5	2
1	2	5	4			3	1	4&5		
1	2	5	4	3		3	1	4&5	2	
1	2&3					3	1	5		
1	2&3	4				3	1	5	2	
1	2&3	4	5			3	1	5	2	4
1	2&3	4&5				3	1	5	2&4	
1	2&3	5				3	1	5	4	

```
1    2&3    5    4          3    1      5    4    2
1    2&3&4                  3    1&2
1    2&3&4  5               3    1&2    4
1    2&3&4&5                3    1&2    4    5
1    2&3&5                  3    1&2    4&5
1    2&3&5  4               3    1&2    5
1    2&4                    3    1&2    5    4
1    2&4    3               3    1&2&4
1    2&4    3    5          3    1&2&4  5
1    2&4    3&5             3    1&2&4&5
1    2&4    5               3    1&2&5
1    2&4    5    3          3    1&2&5  4
1    2&4&5                  3    1&4
1    2&4&5  3               3    1&4    2
1    2&5                    3    1&4    2    5
1    2&5    3               3    1&4    2&5
1    2&5    3    4          3    1&4    5
1    2&5    3&4             3    1&4    5    2
1    2&5    4               3    1&4&5
1    2&5    4    3          3    1&4&5  2
1    3                      3    1&5
1    3    2                 3    1&5    2
1    3    2    4            3    1&5    2    4
1    3    2    4    5       3    1&5    2&4
1    3    2    4&5          3    1&5    4
1    3    2    5            3    1&5    4    2
1    3    2    5    4       3    2
1    3    2&4               3    2      1
1    3    2&4    5          3    2      1    4
1    3    2&4&5             3    2      1    4    5
1    3    2&5               3    2      1    4&5
1    3    2&5    4          3    2      1    5
1    3    4                 3    2      1    5    4
1    3    4    2            3    2      1&4
1    3    4    2    5       3    2      1&4    5
1    3    4    2&5          3    2      1&4&5
1    3    4    5            3    2      1&5
```

1	3	4	5	2		3	2	1&5	4
1	3	4&5				3	2	4	
1	3	4&5	2			3	2	4	1
1	3	5				3	2	4	1	5
1	3	5	2			3	2	4	1&5
1	3	5	2	4		3	2	4	5
1	3	5	2&4			3	2	4	5	1
1	3	5	4			3	2	4&5	
1	3	5	4	2		3	2	4&5	1
1	3&4					3	2	5	
1	3&4	2				3	2	5	1
1	3&4	2	5			3	2	5	1	4
1	3&4	2&5				3	2	5	1&4
1	3&4	5				3	2	5	4
1	3&4	5	2			3	2	5	4	1
1	3&4&5					3	2&4		
1	3&4&5	2				3	2&4	1	
1	3&5					3	2&4	1	5
1	3&5	2				3	2&4	1&5	
1	3&5	2	4			3	2&4	5	
1	3&5	2&4				3	2&4	5	1
1	3&5	4				3	2&4&5		
1	3&5	4	2			3	2&4&5	1	
1	4					3	2&5		
1	4	2				3	2&5	1	
1	4	2	3			3	2&5	1	4
1	4	2	3	5		3	2&5	1&4	
1	4	2	3&5			3	2&5	4	
1	4	2	5			3	2&5	4	1
1	4	2	5	3		3	4		
1	4	2&3				3	4	1	
1	4	2&3	5			3	4	1	2
1	4	2&3&5				3	4	1	2	5
1	4	2&5				3	4	1	2&5
1	4	2&5	3			3	4	1	5
1	4	3				3	4	1	5	2

1	4	3	2			3	4	1&2		
1	4	3	2	5		3	4	1&2	5	
1	4	3	2&5			3	4	1&2&5		
1	4	3	5			3	4	1&5		
1	4	3	5	2		3	4	1&5	2	
1	4	3&5				3	4	2		
1	4	3&5	2			3	4	2	1	
1	4	5				3	4	2	1	5
1	4	5	2			3	4	2	1&5	
1	4	5	2	3		3	4	2	5	
1	4	5	2&3			3	4	2	5	1
1	4	5	3			3	4	2&5		
1	4	5	3	2		3	4	2&5	1	
1	4&5					3	4	5		
1	4&5	2				3	4	5	1	
1	4&5	2	3			3	4	5	1	2
1	4&5	2&3				3	4	5	1&2	
1	4&5	3				3	4	5	2	
1	4&5	3	2			3	4	5	2	1
1	5					3	4&5			
1	5	2				3	4&5	1		
1	5	2	3			3	4&5	1	2	
1	5	2	3	4		3	4&5	1&2		
1	5	2	3&4			3	4&5	2		
1	5	2	4			3	4&5	2	1	
1	5	2	4	3		3	5			
1	5	2&3				3	5	1		
1	5	2&3	4			3	5	1	2	
1	5	2&3&4				3	5	1	2	4
1	5	2&4				3	5	1	2&4	
1	5	2&4	3			3	5	1	4	
1	5	3				3	5	1	4	2
1	5	3	2			3	5	1&2		
1	5	3	2	4		3	5	1&2	4	
1	5	3	2&4			3	5	1&2&4		
1	5	3	4			3	5	1&4		
1	5	3	4	2		3	5	1&4	2	

1	5	3&4			3	5	2		
1	5	3&4	2		3	5	2	1	
1	5	4			3	5	2	1	4
1	5	4	2		3	5	2	1&4	
1	5	4	2	3	3	5	2	4	
1	5	4	2&3		3	5	2	4	1
1	5	4	3		3	5	2&4		
1	5	4	3	2	3	5	2&4	1	
1&2					3	5	4		
1&2	3				3	5	4	1	
1&2	3	4			3	5	4	1	2
1&2	3	4	5		3	5	4	1&2	
1&2	3	4&5			3	5	4	2	
1&2	3	5			3	5	4	2	1
1&2	3	5	4		3&4				
1&2	3&4				3&4	1			
1&2	3&4	5			3&4	1	2		
1&2	3&4&5				3&4	1	2	5	
1&2	3&5				3&4	1	2&5		
1&2	3&5	4			3&4	1	5		
1&2	4				3&4	1	5	2	
1&2	4	3			3&4	1&2			
1&2	4	3	5		3&4	1&2	5		
1&2	4	3&5			3&4	1&2&5			
1&2	4	5			3&4	1&5			
1&2	4	5	3		3&4	1&5	2		
1&2	4&5				3&4	2			
1&2	4&5	3			3&4	2	1		
1&2	5				3&4	2	1	5	
1&2	5	3			3&4	2	1&5		
1&2	5	3	4		3&4	2	5		
1&2	5	3&4			3&4	2	5	1	
1&2	5	4			3&4	2&5			
1&2	5	4	3		3&4	2&5	1		
1&2&3					3&4	5			
1&2&3	4				3&4	5	1		

```
1&2&3   4      5            3&4   5      1      2
1&2&3   4&5                 3&4   5      1&2
1&2&3   5                   3&4   5      2
1&2&3   5      4            3&4   5      2      1
1&2&3&4                     3&4&5
1&2&3&4 5                   3&4&5  1
1&2&3&4&5                   3&4&5  1      2
1&2&3&5                     3&4&5  1&2
1&2&3&5 4                   3&4&5  2
1&2&4                       3&4&5  2      1
1&2&4   3                   3&5
1&2&4   3      5            3&5   1
1&2&4   3&5                 3&5   1      2
1&2&4   5                   3&5   1      2      4
1&2&4   5      3            3&5   1      2&4
1&2&4&5                     3&5   1      4
1&2&4&5 3                   3&5   1      4      2
1&2&5                       3&5   1&2
1&2&5   3                   3&5   1&2    4
1&2&5   3      4            3&5   1&2&4
1&2&5   3&4                 3&5   1&4
1&2&5   4                   3&5   1&4    2
1&2&5   4      3            3&5   2
1&3                         3&5   2      1
1&3     2                   3&5   2      1      4
1&3     2      4            3&5   2      1&4
1&3     2      4      5     3&5   2      4
1&3     2      4&5          3&5   2      4      1
1&3     2      5            3&5   2&4
1&3     2      5      4     3&5   2&4    1
1&3     2&4                 3&5   4
1&3     2&4    5            3&5   4      1
1&3     2&4&5               3&5   4      1      2
1&3     2&5                 3&5   4      1&2
1&3     2&5    4            3&5   4      2
1&3     4                   3&5   4      2      1
1&3     4      2            4
```

1&3	4	2	5		4	1		
1&3	4	2&5			4	1	2	
1&3	4	5			4	1	2	3
1&3	4	5	2		4	1	2	3 5
1&3	4&5				4	1	2	3&5
1&3	4&5	2			4	1	2	5
1&3	5				4	1	2	5 3
1&3	5	2			4	1	2&3	
1&3	5	2	4		4	1	2&3 5	
1&3	5	2&4			4	1	2&3&5	
1&3	5	4			4	1	2&5	
1&3	5	4	2		4	1	2&5 3	
1&3&4					4	1	3	
1&3&4	2				4	1	3	2
1&3&4	2	5			4	1	3	2 5
1&3&4	2&5				4	1	3	2&5
1&3&4	5				4	1	3	5
1&3&4	5	2			4	1	3	5 2
1&3&4&5					4	1	3&5	
1&3&4&5 2					4	1	3&5 2	
1&3&5					4	1	5	
1&3&5	2				4	1	5	2
1&3&5	2	4			4	1	5	2 3
1&3&5	2&4				4	1	5	2&3
1&3&5	4				4	1	5	3
1&3&5	4	2			4	1	5	3 2
1&4					4	1&2		
1&4	2				4	1&2	3	
1&4	2	3			4	1&2	3	5
1&4	2	3	5		4	1&2	3&5	
1&4	2	3&5			4	1&2	5	
1&4	2	5			4	1&2	5	3
1&4	2	5	3		4	1&2&3		
1&4	2&3				4	1&2&3	5	
1&4	2&3	5			4	1&2&3&5		
1&4	2&3&5				4	1&2&5		

1&4	2&5			4	1&2&5	3		
1&4	2&5	3		4	1&3			
1&4	3			4	1&3	2		
1&4	3	2		4	1&3	2	5	
1&4	3	2	5	4	1&3	2&5		
1&4	3	2&5		4	1&3	5		
1&4	3	5		4	1&3	5	2	
1&4	3	5	2	4	1&3&5			
1&4	3&5			4	1&3&5	2		
1&4	3&5	2		4	1&5			
1&4	5			4	1&5	2		
1&4	5	2		4	1&5	2	3	
1&4	5	2	3	4	1&5	2&3		
1&4	5	2&3		4	1&5	3		
1&4	5	3		4	1&5	3	2	
1&4	5	3	2	4	2			
1&4&5				4	2	1		
1&4&5	2			4	2	1	3	
1&4&5	2	3		4	2	1	3	5
1&4&5	2&3			4	2	1	3&5	
1&4&5	3			4	2	1	5	
1&4&5	3	2		4	2	1	5	3
1&5				4	2	1&3		
1&5	2			4	2	1&3	5	
1&5	2	3		4	2	1&3&5		
1&5	2	3	4	4	2	1&5		
1&5	2	3&4		4	2	1&5	3	
1&5	2	4		4	2	3		
1&5	2	4	3	4	2	3	1	
1&5	2&3			4	2	3	1	5
1&5	2&3	4		4	2	3	1&5	
1&5	2&3&4			4	2	3	5	
1&5	2&4			4	2	3	5	1
1&5	2&4	3		4	2	3&5		
1&5	3			4	2	3&5	1	
1&5	3	2		4	2	5		
1&5	3	2	4	4	2	5	1	

1&5	3	2&4		
1&5	3	4		
1&5	3	4	2	
1&5	3&4			
1&5	3&4	2		
1&5	4			
1&5	4	2		
1&5	4	2	3	
1&5	4	2&3		
1&5	4	3		
1&5	4	3	2	
2				
2	1			
2	1	3		
2	1	3	4	
2	1	3	4	5
2	1	3	4&5	
2	1	3	5	
2	1	3	5	4
2	1	3&4		
2	1	3&4	5	
2	1	3&4&5		
2	1	3&5		
2	1	3&5	4	
2	1	4		
2	1	4	3	
2	1	4	3	5
2	1	4	3&5	
2	1	4	5	
2	1	4	5	3
2	1	4&5		
2	1	4&5	3	
2	1	5		
2	1	5	3	
2	1	5	3	4
2	1	5	3&4	

4	2	5	1	3
4	2	5	1&3	
4	2	5	3	
4	2	5	3	1
4	2&3			
4	2&3	1		
4	2&3	1	5	
4	2&3	1&5		
4	2&3	5		
4	2&3	5	1	
4	2&3&5			
4	2&3&5	1		
4	2&5			
4	2&5	1		
4	2&5	1	3	
4	2&5	1&3		
4	2&5	3		
4	2&5	3	1	
4	3			
4	3	1		
4	3	1	2	
4	3	1	2	5
4	3	1	2&5	
4	3	1	5	
4	3	1	5	2
4	3	1&2		
4	3	1&2	5	
4	3	1&2&5		
4	3	1&5		
4	3	1&5	2	
4	3	2		
4	3	2	1	
4	3	2	1	5
4	3	2	1&5	
4	3	2	5	
4	3	2	5	1

2	1	5	4		4	3	2&5		
2	1	5	4	3	4	3	2&5	1	
2	1&3				4	3	5		
2	1&3	4			4	3	5	1	
2	1&3	4	5		4	3	5	1	2
2	1&3	4&5			4	3	5	1&2	
2	1&3	5			4	3	5	2	
2	1&3	5	4		4	3	5	2	1
2	1&3&4				4	3&5			
2	1&3&4	5			4	3&5	1		
2	1&3&4&5				4	3&5	1	2	
2	1&3&5				4	3&5	1&2		
2	1&3&5	4			4	3&5	2		
2	1&4				4	3&5	2	1	
2	1&4	3			4	5			
2	1&4	3	5		4	5	1		
2	1&4	3&5			4	5	1	2	
2	1&4	5			4	5	1	2	3
2	1&4	5	3		4	5	1	2&3	
2	1&4&5				4	5	1	3	
2	1&4&5	3			4	5	1	3	2
2	1&5				4	5	1&2		
2	1&5	3			4	5	1&2	3	
2	1&5	3	4		4	5	1&2&3		
2	1&5	3&4			4	5	1&3		
2	1&5	4			4	5	1&3	2	
2	1&5	4	3		4	5	2		
2	3				4	5	2	1	
2	3	1			4	5	2	1	3
2	3	1	4		4	5	2	1&3	
2	3	1	4	5	4	5	2	3	
2	3	1	4&5		4	5	2	3	1
2	3	1	5		4	5	2&3		
2	3	1	5	4	4	5	2&3	1	
2	3	1&4			4	5	3		
2	3	1&4	5		4	5	3	1	
2	3	1&4&5			4	5	3	1	2

2	3	1&5			4	5	3	1&2
2	3	1&5	4		4	5	3	2
2	3	4			4	5	3	2	1
2	3	4	1		4&5			
2	3	4	1	5	4&5	1		
2	3	4	1&5		4&5	1	2	
2	3	4	5		4&5	1	2	3
2	3	4	5	1	4&5	1	2&3	
2	3	4&5			4&5	1	3	
2	3	4&5	1		4&5	1	3	2
2	3	5			4&5	1&2		
2	3	5	1		4&5	1&2	3	
2	3	5	1	4	4&5	1&2&3		
2	3	5	1&4		4&5	1&3		
2	3	5	4		4&5	1&3	2	
2	3	5	4	1	4&5	2		
2	3&4				4&5	2	1	
2	3&4	1			4&5	2	1	3
2	3&4	1	5		4&5	2	1&3	
2	3&4	1&5			4&5	2	3	
2	3&4	5			4&5	2	3	1
2	3&4	5	1		4&5	2&3		
2	3&4&5				4&5	2&3	1	
2	3&4&5	1			4&5	3		
2	3&5				4&5	3	1	
2	3&5	1			4&5	3	1	2
2	3&5	1	4		4&5	3	1&2	
2	3&5	1&4			4&5	3	2	
2	3&5	4			4&5	3	2	1
2	3&5	4	1		5			
2	4				5	1		
2	4	1			5	1	2	
2	4	1	3		5	1	2	3
2	4	1	3	5	5	1	2	3	4
2	4	1	3&5		5	1	2	3&4
2	4	1	5		5	1	2	4

2	4	1	5	3		5	1	2	4	3
2	4	1&3				5	1	2&3		
2	4	1&3	5			5	1	2&3	4	
2	4	1&3&5				5	1	2&3&4		
2	4	1&5				5	1	2&4		
2	4	1&5	3			5	1	2&4	3	
2	4	3				5	1	3		
2	4	3	1			5	1	3	2	
2	4	3	1	5		5	1	3	2	4
2	4	3	1&5			5	1	3	2&4	
2	4	3	5			5	1	3	4	
2	4	3	5	1		5	1	3	4	2
2	4	3&5				5	1	3&4		
2	4	3&5	1			5	1	3&4	2	
2	4	5				5	1	4		
2	4	5	1			5	1	4	2	
2	4	5	1	3		5	1	4	2	3
2	4	5	1&3			5	1	4	2&3	
2	4	5	3			5	1	4	3	
2	4	5	3	1		5	1	4	3	2
2	4&5					5	1&2			
2	4&5	1				5	1&2	3		
2	4&5	1	3			5	1&2	3	4	
2	4&5	1&3				5	1&2	3&4		
2	4&5	3				5	1&2	4		
2	4&5	3	1			5	1&2	4	3	
2	5					5	1&2&3			
2	5	1				5	1&2&3	4		
2	5	1	3			5	1&2&3&4			
2	5	1	3	4		5	1&2&4			
2	5	1	3&4			5	1&2&4	3		
2	5	1	4			5	1&3			
2	5	1	4	3		5	1&3	2		
2	5	1&3				5	1&3	2	4	
2	5	1&3	4			5	1&3	2&4		
2	5	1&3&4				5	1&3	4		
2	5	1&4				5	1&3	4	2	

2	5	1&4	3	
2	5	3		
2	5	3	1	
2	5	3	1	4
2	5	3	1&4	
2	5	3	4	
2	5	3	4	1
2	5	3&4		
2	5	3&4	1	
2	5	4		
2	5	4	1	
2	5	4	1	3
2	5	4	1&3	
2	5	4	3	
2	5	4	3	1
2&3				
2&3	1			
2&3	1	4		
2&3	1	4	5	
2&3	1	4&5		
2&3	1	5		
2&3	1	5	4	
2&3	1&4			
2&3	1&4	5		
2&3	1&4&5			
2&3	1&5			
2&3	1&5	4		
2&3	4			
2&3	4	1		
2&3	4	1	5	
2&3	4	1&5		
2&3	4	5		
2&3	4	5	1	
2&3	4&5			
2&3	4&5	1		
2&3	5			

5	1&3&4			
5	1&3&4	2		
5	1&4			
5	1&4	2		
5	1&4	2	3	
5	1&4	2&3		
5	1&4	3		
5	1&4	3	2	
5	2			
5	2	1		
5	2	1	3	
5	2	1	3	4
5	2	1	3&4	
5	2	1	4	
5	2	1	4	3
5	2	1&3		
5	2	1&3	4	
5	2	1&3&4		
5	2	1&4		
5	2	1&4	3	
5	2	3		
5	2	3	1	
5	2	3	1	4
5	2	3	1&4	
5	2	3	4	
5	2	3	4	1
5	2	3&4		
5	2	3&4	1	
5	2	4		
5	2	4	1	
5	2	4	1	3
5	2	4	1&3	
5	2	4	3	
5	2	4	3	1
5	2&3			
5	2&3	1		

2&3	5	1			5	2&3	1	4
2&3	5	1	4		5	2&3	1&4	
2&3	5	1&4			5	2&3	4	
2&3	5	4			5	2&3	4	1
2&3	5	4	1		5	2&3&4		
2&3&4					5	2&3&4	1	
2&3&4	1				5	2&4		
2&3&4	1	5			5	2&4	1	
2&3&4	1&5				5	2&4	1	3
2&3&4	5				5	2&4	1&3	
2&3&4	5	1			5	2&4	3	
2&3&4&5					5	2&4	3	1
2&3&4&5	1				5	3		
2&3&5					5	3	1	
2&3&5	1				5	3	1	2
2&3&5	1	4			5	3	1	2	4
2&3&5	1&4				5	3	1	2&4
2&3&5	4				5	3	1	4
2&3&5	4	1			5	3	1	4	2
2&4					5	3	1&2	
2&4	1				5	3	1&2	4
2&4	1	3			5	3	1&2&4	
2&4	1	3	5		5	3	1&4	
2&4	1	3&5			5	3	1&4	2
2&4	1	5			5	3	2	
2&4	1	5	3		5	3	2	1
2&4	1&3				5	3	2	1	4
2&4	1&3	5			5	3	2	1&4
2&4	1&3&5				5	3	2	4
2&4	1&5				5	3	2	4	1
2&4	1&5	3			5	3	2&4	
2&4	3				5	3	2&4	1
2&4	3	1			5	3	4	
2&4	3	1	5		5	3	4	1
2&4	3	1&5			5	3	4	1	2
2&4	3	5			5	3	4	1&2
2&4	3	5	1		5	3	4	2

2&4	3&5			
2&4	3&5	1		
2&4	5			
2&4	5	1		
2&4	5	1	3	
2&4	5	1&3		
2&4	5	3		
2&4	5	3	1	
2&4&5				
2&4&5	1			
2&4&5	1	3		
2&4&5	1&3			
2&4&5	3			
2&4&5	3	1		
2&5				
2&5	1			
2&5	1	3		
2&5	1	3	4	
2&5	1	3&4		
2&5	1	4		
2&5	1	4	3	
2&5	1&3			
2&5	1&3	4		
2&5	1&3&4			
2&5	1&4			
2&5	1&4	3		
2&5	3			
2&5	3	1		
2&5	3	1	4	
2&5	3	1&4		
2&5	3	4		
2&5	3	4	1	
2&5	3&4			
2&5	3&4	1		

5	3	4	2	1
5	3&4			
5	3&4	1		
5	3&4	1	2	
5	3&4	1&2		
5	3&4	2		
5	3&4	2	1	
5	4			
5	4	1		
5	4	1	2	
5	4	1	2	3
5	4	1	2&3	
5	4	1	3	
5	4	1	3	2
5	4	1&2		
5	4	1&2	3	
5	4	1&2&3		
5	4	1&3		
5	4	1&3	2	
5	4	2		
5	4	2	1	
5	4	2	1	3
5	4	2	1&3	
5	4	2	3	
5	4	2	3	1
5	4	2&3		
5	4	2&3	1	
5	4	3		
5	4	3	1	
5	4	3	1	2
5	4	3	1&2	
5	4	3	2	
5	4	3	2	1

About the Author

Douglas Chick is the creator and senior writer for the
computer professionals' E-magazine,
The Network Administrator.com and author of
What All Network Administrators Know

You may contact him at:
DougChick@TheNetworkAdministrator.com